CHANNELING THE
SACRED

ACTIVATING YOUR
CONNECTION TO SOURCE

JO ANN LEVITT

CHANNELING THE SACRED
Activating Your Connection to Source
Edited by Shauna Hardy

SCRIBES OF LIGHT
P R E S S

An Imprint for GracePoint Publishing
(www.GracePointPublishing.com)
In collaboration with Scribes of Light Press of
DivineTransmissions.com
GracePoint Matrix, LLC
322 N Tejon St. #207
Colorado Springs CO 80903
www.GracePointMatrix.com
Email: Admin@GracePointMatrix.com
SAN # 991-6032

Library of Congress Control Number: #2020921501

ISBN-13: (Paperback) *#978-1-951694-23-4*
eISBN: (eBook) *#978-1-951694-22-7*

Books may be purchased for educational, business, or sales promotional use.
For bulk order requests and price schedule contact:
Orders@GracePointPublishing.com

Printed in the United States of America

For more information on Channeling, please visit Jo Ann Levitt online. joannlevitt.com

"How good it is for brothers and sisters to dwell together in Unity Consciousness."

(Adapted from Psalm 133)

"Now is the time to know that all that you do is sacred. Now— why not consider a lasting truce between yourself and God?"

–Hafiz, Sufi Master

Contents

Introduction

Dear Ones,

Everyone has access to transcendental experiences. Nowadays, more and more people have become aware of their connections with Spirit and find this a perfect time to deepen their exploration and knowledge. It is the thirsting for the Divine that draws anyone to a work of this nature.

For that reason, we thank you for your willingness to join us here in this sacred text. Know that you are meeting with Thoth, Ancient Egyptian Wise Counsel as well as Yeshua, more formally known to you as Jesus of Nazareth, along with many other Guides and Light Beings. We are delighted to play with you at this juncture of your three-dimensional world that borders on our Infinite Worlds, which we often refer to as the *Multiverse.* Together with Jo Ann, our scribe, and many other gifted channels and mediums, we are here to explore the nature of channeling and to provide a broad and deep introduction so that you may recognize your own capabilities and tune in to this ancient art as you choose.

You certainly have access. Everyone has access to the Divine. And not just to connect with one Deity. You have access to *all* Wisdom Figures— all Light Beings in Light with whom you are called to interact. And many have already been communicating with you for ages.

But to channel in consistent fashion is a spiritual practice. As with any practice, there are certain steps to follow and methodologies to develop. We present you here with a wide variety of formulas and recipes, exercises and examples, so that eventually you may take off and create your own plans and platforms. Then you will truly discover the delight of channeling.

You may even recognize that you've already been channeling in different ways throughout your life. But now, with this formal introduction and the best and most reliable of blueprints, you'll meet with success, and in a certain way, give rise to the best system, setting, and style that suits your needs.

Jo Ann speaks:

What you are about to read represents the summation of multiple life experiences that have contributed both to an awareness of my spiritual gifts as well as to greater clarity in defining my soul's identity and direction. The art of channeling is a recent arrival and a wondrous experience for me, with surprises at every turn. As I've come to understand it, channeling is indeed a sacred endeavor, often arising after immersion in many types of spiritual practice.

The most recent and most critical influence in my spiritual progress has been my association with Danielle Rama Hoffman (whom you'll meet later in this work) and her team of Divine helpers including Thoth and the Council of Light. To say that meeting up with them was a total game-changer would be a serious understatement. Even to say that my life was turned upside down and the roots of my true Divine heritage revealed would be an understatement. There is absolutely **no way** to adequately describe my *before* and *after* with Danielle, Thoth and the

Divine Transmission team other than to frame the whole experience in this light—I actually ended one whole existence on earth and launched into a totally new life (in the space of these last four years).

Sounds crazy, doesn't it? However, it's not that I was drunk, crazy, or dragging my ball and chain around in living hell before meeting Danielle. On the contrary, I've been on a spiritual path virtually all my life. I was always seeking attunement and the higher life. I grew up Jewish, taught Sunday School and wrote God poetry, then lived eighteen years in an ashram, while searching for deeper roots through Hinduism, Buddhism, and Taoism and finally sought solace in the church, converting to Christianity. Hearing the name Yahweh or Shiva or Yeshua would send me into a spasm of God-realization.

However, it took a while to reach this ecstatic place of connection through the pursuit of many different roles, trainings, and endeavors. Working first as an American history teacher in West Philly and later as an RN at Temple Hospital, having decimated a marriage and several relationships, I was searching for meaning and connection. In my late twenties, I got an invitation from another nurse to take a yoga class in a small town outside Philly called Sumneytown. That was a real turning point. It took the next eighteen years of my life to grow into what I would call a fully communal being. When a friend of mine recently asked me, "What in the world did you get out of living in an ashram?" I answered emphatically: "Community!"

I learned what it means to take care of others and to share and share alike. Read *Acts*, Luke's book in the New Testament to get an early version of true community. From that in-depth experience came the opportunity to learn the meaning of service. Can you imagine eighteen years of living and serving with a group of thirty or forty hippie types while growing a beautiful ashram that later turned into the Kripalu Center for Yoga and Health that accommodates 350 residents? I helped develop and teach the early personal growth programs that drew many seekers, contributing to our brand-new learning center in Massachusetts. However, it was in the earlier years—when I did everything from counseling to cleaning toilets and running the kitchen (not cleaning at the same time as cooking, please!) that I learned the sustaining lessons of *seva* or service. The lasting outcome was that it stripped away resistance I might have had to any kind of work. I still don't encounter resistance to most tasks (unless you ask me to post a pithy paragraph on Facebook).

I became a communal being through ashram living and then I became a Communion-type being when I converted to Christianity and devoted myself to Yeshua's teachings. It's no accident that one of his chief symbols is a Sacred Heart. Diving deeply into that wellspring helped me unearth lifetimes of devotion, with Christ as my true north. When at last I met Danielle, Thoth, and the Council of Light, I accessed an even deeper identity as a Divine co-creator myself, in league with multiple, magnificent, magical Beings! I learned about the interaction between Light Beings in Light and those of us who are Light Beings incarnate! From a heavily focused three-dimensional existence, you might say that I finally found my place inclusive of both Heaven and of Earth!

In 2016, I spotted Danielle's *Council of Light* book in a Great Barrington bookstore in Massachusetts. I read it voraciously, not once but several times. I remember weeping copiously the first time Thoth spoke about being divinely matched. I had no idea that was what I'd craved so deeply in life. By 2017, I had gathered a group of friends and meditators to form a book group, studying the principles of both the *Council of Light* and later the *Tablets of Light*, while meditating and feeling Thoth's energy dance around us. By 2018, we were knee-deep in meditation watching the monthly Energy trend videos that Danielle channels, and by the Great Pandemic of 2020, we'd begun meeting up for what we lovingly called "Tea n' Thoth," (though admittedly no tea could be served on Zoom.)

Spending two consecutive years in Thoth's Magic Academy—a daily immersion in Thoth's transmissions, along with monthly magical calls—helped to heighten my awareness of slower versus speedier vibrations and helped me achieve clear cognizance and recognition of the workings of Unity Consciousness. When I finally landed in Southern France in the fall of 2019 for the Divine Light Activation series, I had the surprise of my life. Making contact with the energetic presence of both Yeshua and Thoth while meditating in a sweet little chapel, I received an *etheric* download to scribe a new Gospel! The image of a white banner scrolled across my mind, its words printed in bright red, "*The 21ˢᵗ Century Gospel of Jesus Christ*—as told to Jo Ann Levitt" and I was shocked. To paraphrase a famous saying, "The rest, they say, is mystery…" (Of course, also history.)

In the space of this past year, with help from my Guides, I will have completed four different volumes, all channeled work. The first, of course, was the *21ˢᵗ Century Gospel.*

The second entitled *El Evangelio* was its Spanish translation. The third came out in April of 2020: a book of rhymed prayers and poems called *Prayers for the Pandemic.* And the fourth book is in your hands:

Channeling the Sacred. The beauty of this process is that every stage was both a precursor to and an absolutely necessary preparation for the next stage of my soul's development.

I stand here now at the pinnacle, recognizing how amazingly timely, amazingly resonant, and amazingly well-matched I am now with Spirit. I have received all the gifts of my longing. I have learned the precious art of communicating deeply with Spirit and have received the deep nectar of Communion. What has emerged as a compilation of those prior stages of growth has its emphasis, however, in *community*. For channeling is no solitary act. Neither is living the true spiritual life. All of us need to surround and immerse ourselves in community—to recognize and draw out the very best of what we hold in common— which is our uniquely Divine heritage.

Chapter One

The Nature of Channeling

The Guides speak:

What Exactly is Channeling?

In the old context, a channel was a causeway or narrow path connecting one area with another, often composed of water, such as the English Channel. Next, it became a source of programming or means to access different information—as with someone asking you to please "change the channel" on the TV (but of course you can't, because the remote fell behind the couch…).

So, if a channel is a causeway, a connector or a means to access new information, then it stands to reason that a human being can be all those things and thus serve as a channel as well. Whether you call that person a medium, a psychic, or a channel makes no difference—all have access to divine wisdom. However, a medium may focus more on information from Ancestors or relatives who've recently passed, whereas Guides may be more attuned to universalities – principles and awareness that leap beyond the margins of space and time as you know them. We come to you in the here and now to explore what is relevant at this stage of your growth, what you may be acknowledging within yourself and what (at the same time) has truly timeless application! (Yeshua loves to hear timeless plays on words…)

What's *Sacred* about it?

If you define *Sacred* as something that is set apart or consecrated for holy purposes, then you have an idea of this channeling. To venerate or sanctify something or someone—which is part of a Sacrament—is also the way this work is intended. So, the underlying meaning of channeled work is imparting whatever wisdom can be consecrated to your own Holy Purpose or Divine understanding. We further explain the Holy Purpose by distinguishing your path of evolution and soul-growth. Little by little, you are stepping out of the boundary of your long-held limiting thoughts and beliefs. Any communication that helps you do so is sacred. Any communication that restores your sense of Divinity and participation in Unity Consciousness is sacred. Combine all of these together and add in any communications from Source that promote a deepened awareness of your evolutionary nature, and that is what we refer to as channeling the Sacred.

Now, with that being said, please understand that these channeled messages do not arrive like a Holy Writ or some authoritarian doctrine you're unable to dispute. The other part of channeling the Sacred has to do with an equally important condition—you are partner to the process. You choose to join with us. This channeling cannot go on without you, and it is what we refer to then, as a co-creative event. We share together equally in the information exchange. We do not know it all, and neither do you. The author, Jo Ann, likes to add in the fact that this is no high and mighty affair. For her, it's real and down to earth.

Seeking Out Dimensions

In order to understand the nature of channeling, first, grasp what dimensions are. Most people can wrap their minds around the idea of a two-dimensional drawing. You look at the picture of a box and everything is flat (Drawing 1).

The two dimensions visible on the page go up and down and side to side but there is no depth or perspective. It just looks like a flat rectangle. When you add shading or sides to the rectangle however, it suddenly seems to grow off the page and takes its place as a three-dimensional thing (Drawing 2).

It has a front, back, and sides, height, width, and depth. It looks like a box. Of course, this box is only a representation. The actual box containing all the donuts is in the cupboard (unless you've eaten them all).

Like the box, you are a three-dimensional being; and you are also multi-dimensional. If you only lived in your three-dimensional world, you would look to us much the same as your young child's stick figure looks on that piece of paper. However, you have the innate capacity to jump dimensions. You can land in the 4th Dimension, which we summarize as Love or the 5th Dimension, which is essentially Stillness, or move on to communicate with us in the subtler realms of higher dimensions. We exist in so many frames and so many different environments that it would be hard to count the full dimensionality of who (and where) we are. But you have access to it all. And you have been out here playing with us for all time. As Yeshua jokingly puts it, "And for no time at all." That's because time is a dimension that humans relate to. Those of us in Spirit exist outside of and beyond time and space.

How You Jump Dimensions

At the same time, we are happy to bridge the gap. Often, we reach out to you in dreams or while you're engaged with an important project and have crossed the narrow confines of your own mind and emotions. And often, you have jumped dimensions without even realizing you've done so.

Consider if you've been on a road trip—perhaps heading to the beach or the mountains on vacation. You've been driving for more than two hours, and even though you feel awake, you notice an odd sensation—you're simply not all there. That's because in that particular moment you've managed to jump dimensions. If the car in front of you swerved or came to a full stop, you'd immediately jump back into full three-dimensionality. But since things are calm and quiet, you can mostly proceed on automatic and visit with us in alternate realities.

Naturally, the easiest and least complicated time for you to jump dimensions is after falling asleep at night. Nothing else impedes or distracts your attention, unless of course you've had too much to drink or have worries on your mind. But all else being the same, it's an excellent time to charge out of your nighttime bed and join us wherever you feel inclined and with whomever you have abiding contact and connection. This is a precious time for learning, soul visitation, and the restoring and reinventing of your Divine mission and Soul plan on Earth. It does not take away from your body's need for repair and restoration but rather plants everything within the larger context of why you came to Earth and what your greater mission is at this time.

While you may lament the fact that you don't have conscious recall or may not realize how effortlessly you jump dimensions, you do so all the time, checking in with your Guides and galactic co-travelers. Your day and nighttime dreams may surface fragments of multidimensional experience or teachings received from off-planet. And at times of deep introspection and internalized consciousness, you easily shift your dimensional focus in order to converse with us. It just doesn't feel like the kind of conversation you might associate with your ordinary existence. Still, you may convene with Beings of Light in order to ask for help in your earthly sojourn, to clarify your understanding—particularly of experiences that tend to originate off-planet to begin with. Did you ever notice how you suddenly become quiet and calmly centered after steeping in multiple yoga postures or strenuous movements in the morning? Your body has worked hard to deliver you to that intra-state. We could almost call it *interstitial* because you've moved outside of your normal cellular structure to dwell in an in-between or altered state of being, merging somewhere beyond matter in the realm of multidimensional magic.

You Are the Receiver and The Transmitter

Imagine for a moment that you've suddenly received this amazing superpower to tune into every single conversation and exchange going on over the internet. You could expand your bandwidth to such an extent that you could simultaneously perceive EVERYTHING being spoken, sung, sorted out, written, or communicated. Now multiply that a thousand-fold to get a beginning sense of the communications happening throughout the universe. Now multiply it a million-fold. If it seems strangely unimaginable or unquantifiable, that's because, in fact, it is. But at the same time, rejoice in this awareness because it's the self-same reason you have access to and the ability to channel information and knowledge through the conduit of your own being. You are both the receiver and the transmitter. And, you have so much more access than you ever imagined! It's almost as if you function like a magical radio tuner that can draw music from all corners of the Universe! This movement happens through the transmission of energy and light. How exciting to know you can sit right here in your living room, set the dial within yourself, and begin the precious task of communicating inter-dimensionally—or carry out what we lovingly refer to as *Channeling the Sacred*.

Chapter Two

Getting to Know your Guides

The Guides speak:

Yes, But Who Are my Guides?

Ah, that is a good question. What may be running through your mind is the idea that this comes naturally to others but not to you. They may channel so effortlessly or so beautifully or so clearly ensconced in Spirit that you may say, "I don't have a chance in hell of knowing what I should do or how I should channel! You tell me Spirit is whispering in my ear or is right here beside me; yet I feel nothing! I know nothing!" And we say to you: what a perfect place to begin—feeling nothing and knowing nothing! Now, all you need to add into the mix is deep relaxation, and you have come up with the perfect working equation for meeting with your Guides.

All beings have Guides. Some have made their Guides quite famous—Edgar Casey, Esther Hicks, and Jane Roberts—but for most of us the Guides are more modest and speak in a language familiar to us, providing insight, collaboration, and perspective without becoming household names. You have a choice between channeling your Guides consciously or unconsciously, and that's totally up to you. We will add, however, that you can trust in the presence of your Divinely matched helpers in Spirit. In a manner of speaking, they are assigned to you, but they are by no means fixed. As you become aware of the distinctions between energy, frequency, and vibration, you will then recognize that as you grow and evolve, you have access to higher and higher frequencies and vibrations. You emit and attract subtler, deeper levels of light and knowledge. Consider the universal principles, "As above so below" and, "As within so without," and then you realize that your Guides actually change and evolve as you do.

Some may stay with you; others may step down. Some may come in as a result of your higher calling (and we mean this as a double entendre: your *calling* as in vocation and your *calling* as in calling for help!). Our author Jo Ann has cycled through many different Guides and helpers. Forever connected with Yeshua and his circle of Light Beings, she was, however, surprised and delighted to re-discover her longtime association with me, Thoth, which allowed her to access the wisdom teachings of Ancient Egypt. Happily, connections awakened for her when she heard Danielle Rama Hoffman channeling "Thoth's Magic Academy" through the Divine Transmissions course mentioned earlier.

At other times, as we've mentioned before, Guides speak to you in dreams or deep meditation. But it doesn't have to be so rarefied or high-falutin'. You may access precious guidance as you write a letter or a poem. Or paint a picture. Guidance may flow through you while gardening or skiing or cooking. Or out on a leisurely hike—or even in the shower! If you understand once and for all that Consciousness is both continuous and contiguous—that is, near you, within you, and around you—then the mystery of channeling is no longer a mystery. You are channeling, Dear Ones, all the time because of the very NATURE of Consciousness itself.

The yogis maintain three aspects of consciousness that apply to us, captured in the Sanskrit term, *Satchidananda*. Breaking it down, you discover that within consciousness there is a continuous blending and interaction between SAT (Truth), CHIT (Mind-stuff), and ANANDA (Bliss). When you enter deep, compelling meditation, there is a lovely co-mingling between truth, consciousness, and bliss, which deposits you smack in the middle of the Divine. We are not sitting out here on some cloudbank beckoning to you from light-years away. We are, instead, here now, free, available, accessible, and present through the excellent piloting of your very own Truth-Mind-Stuff-Bliss. As Yeshua loves to invite people to gather in, we quote his familiar saying in Scripture: "Come and see!"

The Most Vital Part of Channeling

The most vital part of channeling has to do with your desire. If your desire is strong enough, then you *will* make contact with us. To clarify the role of desire, we invoke the image of a bird that suddenly lands on your front step. But this is no ordinary bird for when you peer more closely, you discover that this poor critter has no wings. You think to yourself, how in the world did it get here? But you willingly tackle the problem to help out this wingless bird, which for the purpose of our discussion is only a teaching tool. In order for our bird to fly, obviously she needs two wings. We'll call one wing *belief*

- to fly she must have a built-in belief that she can do it. But belief alone is insufficient. It will just keep her flapping that one wing. She needs a second wing to create lift, and we call that wing *desire*. She wants to fly and believes she can fly and—whoosh—she's up and away in a nanosecond. The same applies to you for any effect or experience that you wish to manifest. In some instances, you may realize that you have desire without strong belief. No matter. Your desire is the stronger measure and can create the fuel that encompasses belief and lifts you into takeoff. If you have a heartfelt desire to try out channeling, then that strong positive energy itself brings you face-to-face with your innate abilities.

For the purpose of further explanation, we reintroduce the metaphor of that poor wingless bird dropped back on your front step. Once your intention is well placed (meaning that belief and desire are now proven commodities), you can begin to design the working model. To proceed, the bird will again need two wings. Only this time her first wing needs to be *effort*. There is practice and yet again more practice involved. But one wing won't get the channeled bird up in the air, for you must understand that this is a *co-creative* process.

We Light Beings in Light are working hand-in-hand with you. Or as Yeshua prefers to say, "we're working light in light with you," since we have no hands to speak of. Therefore, you bring this wondrous equation to fulfillment when you add the second wing of *surrender*. Your first wing makes contact, asks questions, holds the space, and then through surrender, we arrive.

Whom Will You Channel?

Is it your favorite deity? Will you channel your own bespoke set of Guides? Or seek out historical figures or sacred beings? Or would you prefer to dip into the vast network of consciousness and just let some Being or another—whoever wants to—come through?

You may already be channeling through your daily prayers or meditation. You may have established contact with Light Beings long ago but have not yet recognized what we refer to as their *Signature Energy.* Yeshua has his own private, graceful Signature Energy. It's not the way he signs his name but rather the way he emanates a certain definable glow. People around the globe pray to Yeshua frequently (calling on him with his more common moniker, Jesus) and can sense and feel through connecting to his Signature Energy, when he's actually *dropped in.* And though Thoth from Ancient Egypt is not as well known, he also has a distinct Signature Energy, which you can begin to sensitize yourself to, as his presence is required.

Although Jo Ann has a broad Council of Light Beings who guide and speak to her on different occasions, she is most attuned to what she calls her little triumvirate: Yeshua, Thoth, and Anna (the grandmother of Jesus). All three of us speak through her, but each of us may come forward in different ways, depending on the topic.

In this work that you are reading, our overall purpose is to unravel the meaning of channeling, and to clarify how to access Guides and understand our purpose in co-creating with you. Everyone has Guides. Everyone has messengers from Spirit. If you have arrived at a new vantage point in terms of recognizing this association, then you can make this process of channeling more conscious and deliberate. It is always a choice. What would you choose?

Why Would you Channel?

This is a very good question. If you're not familiar with the practice, it may seem hokey, delusional or a waste of your time. But here we meet up at a crossroads of sorts. The most basic response to the 'why' of channeling boils down to this: you're at a place in your spiritual development where it's important for you to establish a relationship with the Divine. We could say it even better: you're ready to acknowledge the relationship you already have with the Divine and draw more deeply from that connection. Either way there is an exchange of information, new perceptions available, heartfelt guidance, help clearing blocks and resistance, and through the vehicle of channeling, an opening is created for you to step more fully into your divine mission and integrate the nature of your Divine Being more fully into your life.

This last point has been very important for Jo Ann. She was content and at ease in her nicely circumscribed life, whether teaching on the faculty of Kripalu Center or working as a counselor and spiritual healer at Canyon Ranch. Both of those platforms made it easy for her to work diligently and graciously, bringing out more and more of what we refer to as her Zone of Genius. You too will be able to recognize the areas of your expertise—where energy and information flow through you effortlessly and where you receive great joy and inspiration sharing your gifts and talents. Channeling the *21ˢᵗ Century Gospel* as Jo Ann did in 2019 and then stepping up to the plate with this work have taken her to a new (and often uncomfortable) level of being and expression. But that is the result of channeling, receiving divine guidance and direction. There are times in your life when you have already begun traveling a different path, but you're still mesmerized and under the influence of the old way of being. It sometimes takes a few whispered messages (or a broad kick in the butt) to wake up to who you are now and what your life is about.

Chapter Three

Acknowledging the Non-Dual Nature of Reality

The Guides speak:

In a sense all inner work has its basis in the practice of meditation. Meditation provides the platform, or springboard, from which channeling can emerge. We could almost say that while meditation is the ability to witness your own thoughts, channeling is witnessing thoughts from the Divine. Of course, that's a simplification: all channeled process is a blend. But it's a good entry point. Have you, in fact, developed your own meditation practice?

Before diving into a practice of channeling or accessing deeper intuitive knowing, it's helpful to make your acquaintance with those who've been channeling in different types of settings. In the chapters that follow, you will meet up with different psychics and channels who share from the depths of their experience. Each one is markedly different. Yet each one taps into what we call Unity Consciousness—or the non-dual nature of reality. From each person, you may derive a different perspective and a different understanding of what channeling is that hopefully broadens and deepens your insight into and appreciation of the channeling process.

Rev. Suzanne DeWees, Ph.D.

Reverend, Spiritual Healer and Intuitive Counselor

Rev. Suzanne DeWees began her spiritual practice of yoga and meditation in the mid- 1970s and became a founding member of The Kripalu Center for Yoga and Health. By attuning to spirit, she received guidance through the medium of automatic writing in the early 1980's. In time, she channeled spiritual Guides and a spiritual teacher from the non-physical dimension. The foundation of her mediumistic talents lies in Aware Presence.

She has participated in ongoing meditation retreats in the Vipassana and Dzogchen traditions for the past 35 years, has studied with meditation masters in Burma, India, and Nepal, as well as with senior teachers at the Barre Insight Meditation Center, Kripalu Center, and in Thailand. Her studies of Vedanta, the science of non-dual reality, began in 2005 to present.

Suzanne's main focus during a reading includes guidance on awareness, mindfulness, self-healing, spiritual growth, and personal transformation. She allows for a higher perspective to come through from Spirit to look at and deal with life's situations. Suzanne offers spiritual healing and intuitive counseling in her home in Cassadaga, Florida, as well as by Skype, FaceTime, or Zoom. For more information, consult Suzanne's website: www.suzannedewees.com

Suzanne speaks:

First, a brief prayer: I want to take a moment to honor our friendship and the love we share with Spirit, and I invite the Guides to come in and work intimately with us. I also invite any deceased Loved Ones to be part of this conversation - along with Masters and Teachers in the nonphysical dimension - and whatever different lineages or Beings from prior incarnations may assist us in communing with Spirit. We now give ourselves over to this process, learning and unfolding that which is known, and with that I say, 'Amen.'

This is often how I invoke Spirit in an actual channeled session. In some ways the practice of channeling is so simple—it's being connected to Spirit. It's not just the current idea of being with Spirit; it's *being* Spirit. And it may not necessarily mean just channeling Guides; it can also include deceased Loved Ones because I work with them equally.

Despite all the odd notions about channeling, it's not such an unusual or unprecedented event. I'm not going anywhere. I don't need to make a connection. I'm allowing the consciousness that's present and that pervades all of us to be the actual conversation. The dialogue is the shared moment. And I always know that the Guide is there for a reason, or the Loved One is there for a reason. My role is to help facilitate the Loved One's reason or the client's reason for having this conversation. So, it's a three-way Communion. It does, in fact, feel like Communion.

Working With my Guides

The real focus of my Guides is working with clients to help them achieve spiritual maturity and to develop awareness of their innate capacity to evolve—right then and there—through help from the Guides. However, it's interesting that people don't often come with that expectation; in fact, many people want to receive predictions about the future. I find that to be either an area where my channeling is weak, or one in which my Guides aren't interested in providing information because life is so often in flux. Even after a period of three months or so, things can go haywire. That's all it takes. So, I may be able to make a prediction for you for the next three months that's relatively accurate, but beyond that, life changes, people's values change, and often their karma comes into play. So, I really like to stick with what my Guides prefer to focus on—which is relationship with oneself, relationship with the other, based on the relationship with oneself, and in general, the psychology of spiritual development. The basis of that psychology has to do with being present—I must be right here right now as who I am and not in a dream world about myself, or a fantasy about myself.

I can't look at myself as an object. Instead my focus is to be right here as I am and allow the Guides to work with me.

My main method for attuning to my Guides has to do with the ongoing study of reality as non-dual. There are not two separate realities, with the Guides inhabiting one and us in another. It's not two. It's all the Supreme Reality when I allow the grace to be there with the Guides. As I said before, I'm not *going* anywhere; I'm allowing that consciousness to be present. I welcome the Infinite Intelligence to be with me during the session. I also invoke different prayers and continue my non-dual studies when I'm not in a session. And I do a lot to ready myself before the session itself. First of all, my environment has to be impeccably clean, and I am always dressed in a professional manner. Water is available for clients, candles are lit, and the recorder is ready to go. It is a professional presentation, and a professional appearance is important for me and for my clients. I always take care of my own needs in the morning and complete my meditation, so that I'm not rushed. The result is that I'm really ready to receive, or to allow, when the session begins.

I continue to channel the Guide *Monseria*—who describes herself as a Star teacher. She has communicated that she's been helping us on the planet for eons. I had a Guide named *Blessian* with whom I communicated through automatic writing after morning yoga and prayers when I lived at Kripalu Yoga Center. That guide introduced me to *Monseria* in 1982. She's been a constant presence with me since then. She came to me once visually and so I have an image of her in my mind. So unusual—she had lavender eyes! I was having an acupuncture session and she came right up next to the bedside, this beautiful woman, clear as day, and she was dressed in blue. You might picture the kind of blue that Mother Mary would be wearing. I don't remember her hair because her eyes were lavender and stood out, but she remained very close to me and it was just one of those extraordinary moments.

I also had an American Indian Guide come to me with a full headdress on when I was living at the ashram in Summit Station, Pennsylvania, many years before I started automatic writing. I was alone, resting, when all of a sudden, there he was standing at my feet! He looked just like a warrior dressed for battle. I never got a name or a sense of his energy, but I think it was the first time that a Guide had actually showed up. But even before I had come to the ashram, I had a strange virtual experience; I would see a gold bar about four inches wide that would follow me around my apartment. It looked almost the same as an actual bar of gold, only it was an apparition, and a very strange introduction to the world of Spirit.

My channeling has gone through many different stages, and I'm very comfortable with the work. If emotions come up in clients during sessions, I allow people to have their moment and encourage them to be present to their emotions, as it is all part of the healing process. I've also learned to allow space for quiet and contemplation. Although clients often want to talk a lot and tell me their life story, I encourage them to be at ease and even to welcome moments of silence, for things may be brewing beneath the surface. Rather than crowd the session with all kinds of input, I try to make spaciousness a significant aspect of our process, as well as sacredness. I may at times remind the client that although their Loved Ones have gone, they have not gone far.

My key strength as a channel lies in knowing that the Guides are not separate from me. Nor are the deceased relatives or for that matter, the client. I think my key challenge would be to open to the idea of predicting things. I'm not sure if I could get my Guides to work with predictions; it hasn't been their focus in the past. Nor am I really inspired about it because it seems that giving predictions can make people lazy about doing the work themselves. Through all the years that I've been channeling, I haven't focused on trying to get anywhere in particular as a medium. After all is said and done, my main strength is in knowing who I am. And I'm thoroughly supported in this as I've been living in a spiritualist community of psychics and mediums in Florida for twenty-two years. The community itself has been here since 1894. I am certified and permitted to work publicly and privately through the Cassadaga Spiritualist Camp Meeting Association via a rigorous student training process.

Working with Deceased Loved Ones

I am considered clairsentient, which means I'm downloading the information while I'm speaking. I don't have an idea of where I'm going; it's just being given to me as I speak to the client. Loved Ones work a little differently; they just give one or two words or a phrase. And my Guides are so wonderful. They often give me the name of the client's deceased Loved One who is communicating, and this brings reassurance to the client.

I was working with a client one day and the woman's grandfather came through. He called her what sounded to me like "Chickpea," and I asked her if her grandfather called her Chickpea, and she replied, "No. He calls me 'Sweet Pea.'" Sometimes I don't get things exactly; it's as if there's a little static in the airwaves. Another time, a woman's

Loved One came through, and I repeated to her, "He wanted to tell you about the flag." After offering that brief message, that's when I just stop. I let the person tell me what that means. So, this woman started to cry because she had just come from a military funeral, and she had an officially wrapped military flag in her car that she was taking to a veteran's association immediately following our session.

In that case, as in so many others, all I had to do was say one word and then get out of the way and see what it means for the person. If I try to interpret things, I inevitably get in trouble. I'm reminded of another example where a man had made an appointment for a reading not long after his young son had died. Following a brief centering, I opened my eyes, looked at him kindly, and asked, "Are you having an affair?" Hearing that, his jaw dropped. That was the last thing he had come for! But the truth was that he hadn't been able to grieve properly for his son because he was having an affair, and there were some obviously unresolved issues with that since he was still married. So that's what the Guides worked on with him.

There was a very important session that unfolded while I was at a rehabilitation retreat for drug users. I provided healing on a young man, and I felt that his mother was working with us. He was in his twenties. After the healing session, we did a consultation, and I mentioned that I felt like his mother was with us. She gave me three words; she said, "Don't do it." Then I told him about the accompanying vision. In the Florida waterways there are springs that go down very deep into the earth, and I asked him, "Is there any chance you're free-diving into a deep spring? Because this is what I'm seeing, and your mother is saying, 'Don't do it!'" And he responded, "No, those are my dark thoughts. I've been thinking of committing suicide." And then I said to him, "Who is Belinda?" And he said, "That's my grandmother." And I said, "Belinda is right here with your mother. You are not alone. They want you to know that you are not alone." I saw him transform during that 45-minute session, and at the end he looked like a completely different human being. The heavy burden was gone. His countenance was full of light, and the suicidal thoughts were completely dissolved through his mother's presence in spirit and her love and that of his grandmother.

It's interesting, though. When I first started channeling, I did not want to work with deceased Loved Ones. I only wanted to work with Guides whom I thought were smarter, more evolved, and not attached to certain outcomes. However, what I have found is that deceased relatives can help resolve emotional issues, unfinished business, or clarification on cause of death. As much as I love working with Guides and doing intuitive counseling, there are clearly times when deceased relatives are a major source of help. After doing a session with a woman whose husband had died more than a year ago, I received a call from her. She had finally cleaned out his closet and gotten rid of all his clothing and effects. She realized in the session that he was always with her, so she no longer needed to cling to his material things as a reminder of his presence. His love was in her heart. In another session, a man's deceased wife communicated with him evidentially and soon afterwards he reunited with his adult children. Perhaps he let go of guilt in the session.

Sometimes people come with a strong agenda to have a particular deceased relative come through. One time a woman had one person in mind that she wanted to hear from, and although I actually brought through three of her other relatives, she was very disappointed in our session. So, I gave her back her money and told her that this was not a "Dial-a-Spirit" kind of session. It is difficult to work with people who are unrealistic, rude, or condescending. This only happens occasionally, and my Guides are generally very helpful as I can often gain a skeptic's trust with genuine guidance or evidential information. If after ten minutes, I can see it's not a good match, I encourage the client to seek guidance elsewhere.

Regarding current relationships, I have had women get in their car and break up with an abusive boyfriend immediately following a session with me. For the most part, though, the Guides seem to want to preserve marriage, as long as there's no physical abuse involved. In fact, one woman whom I saw recently told me she had gone home a year ago following an intuitive counseling session and boldly stated to her husband, "Suzanne said that I should stay in this marriage, and so I am." Of course, it was the Guides encouraging her to evolve spiritually. She scheduled this recent session to tell me how happy she and her husband were in their marriage to this day.

Getting Out of the Way

My Guides are very specific about who I work with, and I don't think people are sent to me for the most part unless they're prepared to work at a deeper level of transformation within themselves. Most of us go about with an idea of ourselves—of who it is we think we are; and when we don't live up to that idea or concept, we then carry a psychological burden.

My Guides invariably cut to the chase; releasing the self-dissatisfaction that the person is identifying with and working with the actual spirit of the person, honoring their presence and their noble efforts to find happiness. I facilitate that process. The outcome of such deep work is invariably fascinating. People often feel like I'm their best friend when they leave after 45 minutes. I get letters and lots of feedback. I know they feel that I've helped them "see the light", and I'm not even the one doing it. I'm just out of the way. That's what I've learned—my task is simply to get out of the way of my projections, my goals or any aspirations I might have—really, I don't have expectations of myself any longer. And I've had plenty of time to practice; I've been doing this channeled work since 1982. So, the upshot is that I've had a long time to get out of the way.

Chapter Four

How Do You Know What You Know?

Jo Ann speaks:

As Light Beings who happen to be wrapped in physical bodies, we first learn about our world through the five senses of sight, sound, touch, taste, and smell. Think of a baby crawling around putting everything they find into their mouths. Or a toddler who, with the ecstasy of finally locomoting on their two feet, runs back and forth, back and forth, testing the different sensations between carpet and linoleum on their tiny feet.

Now advance that little being another thirty or forty years, and you have a scientist who's asking for demonstrable proof of Spirit—or what we might call evidence-based knowledge. Not that we have anything against science—by any means! However, in this particular era, there seems to be greater dependence on providing logical evidence or some kind of research or data that backs up your theories. As if the evidence beyond your senses can't be relied upon. Well, of course it can't—say phenomenologists. There's no way to validate or replicate the results! Yet, we know otherwise. If you tune in through your sixth sense, you'll have an appreciation for what lies beyond—and you can take it further out by tuning in to your seventh, eighth, or even eighteenth level of consciousness.

All of us have access to deep spiritual knowing, and to insight, intuition, and multiple forms of clairvoyance, whose meaning really boils down to *clear seeing*. Oh, but it's so easy to obfuscate that vision based on what we've been taught growing up, and how we've been conditioned NOT to see. Most of us are urged not to mention the angels, fairies, or weird apparitions that we've seen when we're among polite company. Instead, we're trained out of our supernatural cognition to focus principally on the features of this physical world. Now that has some advantage, of course, mainly having to do with survival. But a vast treasure trove of knowledge may then be withheld from our awareness, though thankfully only as a temporary effect. As we grow, insights and intuitions have a way of bursting through the thin veil of our conditioning, reminding us that there's so much more to be known and experienced in this great Universe of ours.

Thank goodness for the re-emergence of channels and psychics who have had the courage to let insights come through and who stay faithful to their knowledge and intuition. In the remaining part of this chapter you will meet with Ann Elliott—a most extraordinary Light Being—who combines a long business career with her love of intuition and metaphysics. I have been fortunate to attend Ann's high-spirited and very informative class on Intuition.

Ann Elliott

Business Coach, Health & Wellness Innovator, and Intuition Instructor

After leaving a comfortable job in Corporate America in 1996 to start her own business in Supply chain and Logistics, Ann Elliott developed her company, Solertis, which rapidly gained attention for delivering remarkable results and demonstrating an unwavering commitment to her clients' success. Out of that enterprise she gained referrals to top executives at Fortune 500 companies, private equity firms, and ambitious start-ups. In addition, her strong focus in health and wellness set Ann on a different trajectory, creating corporate wellness programs, and later contracting with providers such as the Mayo Clinic, WebMD and the American Heart Association to provide tools and resources benefiting employees while reducing her client companies' escalating costs of healthcare. Through multiple applications of self-care, including yoga practice, Mindfulness meditation, Energy work and her training as a Cranial-sacral practitioner, Ann developed a comprehensive approach to optimal health. In her latest entrepreneurial adventure —AWE & Co — she provides customized wellness and personal development programs, curated and adapted from her own unique approach to health and wellbeing. In addition, the well-kept secret within her corporate work as well as with her individual clients is Ann's uncanny connection to Spirit and her ability to access intuitive knowledge. Flashes of insight and Divine guidance light up her life and work. Thus, from mediation to meditation, she supports individuals and groups toward growth and higher consciousness, using her intuition, her business background, and her leadership experience along with her passion for wellness.

See Ann's website: www.awethenticity.com

Ann speaks:

For many years, I knew I had access to information that I did not learn in school, from the Internet, the news, or from any traditional sources. I did not know the source of this information, but it was very real and mostly accurate. Over many decades, I have grown to trust this wisdom and Divinity and to treat it with great reverence. More recently, I have embraced my ability to help others who are interested in learning how to cultivate and utilize their own intuitive gifts.

After teaching Mindfulness and other wellness-related practices to a variety of audiences, I wanted to teach something entirely of my own creation. I have always loved and utilized my intuition, so I created "Intuition Masterclass: *Mystery, Mastery and Mechanics.*" In that course, I encourage participants to consider what constitutes Intuition and how we may each make use of it in our daily lives. The dictionary simply defines Intuition as the "ability to acquire knowledge without recourse to conscious reasoning." I find it to be a bit more complex and nuanced. Over decades, I have refined my intuitive system and have created courses to encourage others to develop their unique style. As part of my teaching, I often provide examples and stories to help others discover and cultivate their own intuitive capabilities. Here is one of those stories....

David, Edward, and the Case of the Missing Passport

My closest friends are aware of my intuitive capabilities and occasionally ask to engage them when they are in a jam. Several summers back, my dear college friend, David, was soon to be married and I was planning to attend the ceremony in Colorado. David called a few weeks before the wedding and said that his fiancée, Jenny, had misplaced her passport during the move into their new home and he wondered if I could help find it before their honeymoon. I asked David a few questions and then told him I would call him back after doing an intuitive read.

During the phone call with David, Edward, the man I was dating at the time, was sitting near enough to overhear the conversation.

Edward was surprised I would think myself capable of providing such intuitive assistance and was skeptical that anything like locating a missing passport was possible. With a business brain predisposed to intellectual, scientifically validated facts, Edward thought it would be fun to test my capabilities, so he challenged me to identify the location of his passport.

Over the years, I have developed and refined an intuitive process that works for me. I continue to hone it and discover nuances, but the fundamentals are as follows. First, if I am seeking some specific information, I drop *any* expectation that I will get anything. I release any need to be "right," I let go of attachment to the outcome and get very quiet. Because intuition is a gift, I treat it with reverence, so I ask inside myself if this is an acceptable use of my gift? Once I feel the 'nod' to proceed with my intuitive process, I formulate my question and release the question as though seeing it drift off weightlessly into the cosmos.

In this case, I simply closed my eyes and asked the location of Edward's passport. As I waited, I maintained a position of receptivity and non-attachment with relaxed curiosity. In this case, my awareness shifted to an image I recognized - Edward's home office – a place I had often visited. I viewed the scene as though it was the set of a theatrical play and I am in the position of the audience. This perspective represents detachment and objectivity—as I am the viewer rather than a participant in the scene. I continued to view the scene and as I did, my attention shifted to something in the far corner of the office on a flat surface beneath a bookshelf. I watched as that focal point started to move in a kangaroo-like motion out of Edward's office, down the hallway and out his front door.

Still in a state of receptivity and relaxed curiosity, I paused, feeling that my process was not entirely complete – even though the focal point had moved beyond my perspective. Suddenly, I viewed the same kangaroo-like motion enter back into Edward's office and the focus of my attention came to rest in the back corner of the office where the motion started. At this point, I felt the process was complete although I do not logically understand what I had been seeing. When I opened my eyes and described what I've observed, Edward instantly lapsed into a long seizure of howling laughter. Apparently, the focal point I had keyed into was the exact spot where Edward keeps his briefcase. And inside was his passport! Thus, his passport traveled inside the briefcase to work and to other places and then returned to the spot where he keeps his briefcase in his home office. I had no conscious knowledge of this. In this case as with my process in general, I shared my observations because that often helps me to interpret, validate and utilize the intuition I've received, like putting together pieces of a puzzle.

In courses I teach and in my work with clients, I emphasize our responsibility to use intuition in service to humanity and for the greater good of all. Intuition is part of our journey along an evolutionary spiral toward higher states of consciousness; thus, I treat it with reverence. Being neutral and objective also strengthens intuitive accuracy. If you are attached or emotionally invested in an outcome, it creates a distortion in the flow and veracity of intuition.

Being Grounded

To receive and translate information from beyond the five senses most effectively, it helps to be grounded. Being grounded has many different meanings and in this instance, I mean being fully present in your body;

acknowledging your thoughts and feelings while not being overly attached to them. While often entertaining, intuitive insights are most valuable when they can be translated into something meaningful, purposeful, or actionable, and that requires being fully present in this dimension.

Mindfulness and other meditative disciplines offer suggestions for being present and grounded. Doing such practices regularly is great for health and wellbeing and also for accessing your intuition. The following is a practice I use for myself as well as with clients and groups.

Practice for Grounding

In a comfortable seated position, relax your shoulders, jaw, and neck. Close your eyes and feel the weight of your body in the chair.

Feel the places where your body is making contact with the chair or the floor.

This is your time to be entirely present to yourself. There's nowhere to go—nothing to do. Just be here.

Allowing your focus to move to your breath, let any distractions fade into the background.

On the in breath, slowly breathe in joy, peace, love, and light.

On the out breath, release anything that is no longer serving you.

Pause for a moment.

On the in breath, slowly breathe in joy, peace, love, light and gratitude. On the out breath, release anything that is no longer serving you. Toxins, emotions, thoughts, carbon dioxide… anything you no longer need.

Tune in and feel more of the weight of your feet on the floor.

Settle more deeply into the chair, noticing a sense of simplicity and ease in just being here.

On the in breath, slowly breathe in joy, peace, love, and light.

On the out breath, release anything that no longer serves you.

Allow your awareness to travel to the base of your spine and then let it drop deep, deep into the heart of Mother Earth.

And on the in breath, slowly breathe in joy, peace, love, and light.

On the out breath, release anything that you no longer need.

In a deep state of connection with the heart of the Earth, continue to breathe in joy, peace, love and light and allow that to drop down into the Earth and through all the planetary grids.

On the out breath, release anything that no longer serves you.

Maintaining this deep connection, continue to share joy, peace, love and light with the Earth as you come back to yourself in the chair. As you continue to be held in this beautiful, relaxed serenity, return to your normal state of awareness here and now.

Chapter Five

Are You Ready to Begin?

The Guides speak:

Are you Ready to Begin?

It is helpful to dive in and experiment before you draw conclusions about your capacity to do channeled work. Many of us have overlays or illusory patterns and limiting beliefs about our abilities. Ideas occur, such as: I'm not good enough, spiritual enough, advanced enough, deserving enough, well-versed enough, capable enough...you name it! We tend to rely upon these thoughts to keep from wandering out beyond our comfort zone. On the other hand, could you imagine bragging about these abilities or calling attention to yourself? Where might you take a bow? To whom would you willingly acknowledge that you are in the habit of channeling entities from the Divine? We're being a bit facetious, but you can understand the notion of limits, especially as they arise as a result of repeated (antiquated) thought patterns. That is why we urge you to speak to your old limiting beliefs and simply wave them on. If you wish, you can acknowledge their departure with the familiar phrase, "Thank you for sharing..."

Grounding is Next

Using Ann's careful directions from Chapter Four, take time to center yourself and to experience the full benefit of a grounding exercise. You may find upon completion that you know exactly where you want to go next. You may find that journaling certain flashes of insight or messages from Spirit are what call to you now. Or you may feel that you want to sit for a longer period and just drink in the silence. Take time and allow intuition itself to be your Guide.

First Experiment

Now consider taking on a new kind of experiment. For the first round, we recommend you create a virtual chat with someone on the earthly plane. There's a simple reason for this—first of all, you're already acquainted; you have some idea of the way they tend to think. Secondly, because it's someone in human form, it's easy to bring them into your imagination and you may even find that you receive some benefit from clearing any concerns or conflict between you. So, choose someone you know and someone whom you'd like to converse with. Although you may decide to do this experiment in writing, our recommendation is to practice speaking out loud at first. You'll find that the technology of channeling lands more clearly as a result. Once having spoken out loud, it's easy to then translate this process into written practice.

Procedure:

1. Find a place where you can sit comfortably and speak out loud without being disturbed or distracted.

2. Take a few minutes to enter a calm or meditative state. You may engage breath-work, focused prayer, Ann's grounding exercise, or whatever your favorite means for entering the silence.

3. Invite in the energetic presence of the person you wish to channel.

4. Set your intention out loud for the purpose of this session, mentioning what you hope to learn or to accomplish.

5. It may help to set a chair or cushion as "place-holder" or light a candle—anything that helps prepare the space to invite in their presence.

6. Begin to imagine them with you. Sense and feel the quality of energy, the general emotional state, and the way you feel when you're together.

7. Acknowledge and thank the person for their willingness to be here and to work on this channeling agenda with you. You may ask a question, present a concern, look for support or understanding, or receive input on an important decision.

8. If you like, it is actually helpful in the beginning to move out of your seat and sit in the chair or designated place you've set aside when you wish to channel or receive information from their point of view. (This particular design originated with Gestalt therapy and has great relevance here.)

9. Trust that you may receive and speak on the person's behalf. Allow them to have their say, to state what's on their mind or to let you in on their point of view. You may be surprised about how much information is channeled through you.

10. Returning to your seat, pick up the thread of the conversation, and respond from your own point of view.

11. In this way, allow yourself to move back and forth, taking up each part, divulging more and more of yourself and more and more of the other's self. Don't be surprised if you learn

from both sides of the coin. And don't be surprised if different emotions surface. Allow whatever comes up to be accepted and fully expressed.

12. Continue the interview until you finally achieve a sense of closure, peace, or integration.

Congratulate yourself—that was a fine piece of channeling and who knew you could learn so much through this admittedly strange methodology?

Other Methods

There are obviously numerous and varied ways to access spiritual knowledge and insight. Sometimes it helps to be in the presence of others who are adept at the practice of channeling. Sometimes, soft music playing in the background helps you release excess focus on the earthly plane. Take time to play with this process. There's no right or wrong way to channel, there's what appeals to you and what occurs effortlessly (after some time devoted to practice). Also, allow it to develop slowly! It takes time to be at ease sending and receiving messages from Spirit. It also takes time to trust the veracity of what you are receiving. So be patient with the process, allowing it to unfold in its own way and with its own innate and perfect timing.

Why Channeling Works

Channeling is a natural phenomenon that has been with us for all time. Since we call ourselves Beings of Light, it's because we are literally made of light—whether embodied as beings or not. Could you envision yourself as a pulsating series of light waves, or as particles of light? When you touch your nose or your belly, you meet up with material substance. It's pushing it to consider yourself as light, with your matter broken down to its primal constituent parts. However, that's what we see when we observe you. You are radiant light. So are we.

Although you may not realize it, light has the amazing capacity to convey packets of information within its beams. That is the basis for all types of information sharing that go on in this and parallel worlds. It's not just the spoken word. It can happen in images. An artist may see a rose or a hummingbird and immediately translate them through a condensed packet of light into a montage of beautiful images painted on canvas. For a composer, a hummed melody translates into specific notes, lyrics, or an amazing orchestral piece. An engineer might suddenly envision steel beams rebalanced in the most efficient way to support a structure. But invariably light is the medium that carries the message.

So light is what we're made of and light is our means to convey information. If you're a massage therapist, imagine that your carrier oil is the equivalent of light; it conveys the healing benefits of the essential oils you're using by delivering through the medium of that oil. For a writer, any message you wish to convey—even digital ones—are delivered through light: light within light within light. You are so immersed in this magic substance that like water for the proverbial fish, you have no idea it's the perfect environment to swim in.

Frequencies and Vibrations

Channeling is thus a more conscious use of your light frequencies and vibrations. Think of a scale with the low to higher range of sounds. Most sounds of music vibrate their way to your eardrums, but then there are sounds that only your dog can hear. Like light, sound contains vibrations and frequencies. Likewise, translate that into light, and you have variable frequencies from very low to extremely high ranges where your own eyes cannot go. But you have sense perception far beyond your eyes. And when you learn to entrain with the higher frequencies and vibrations, then you receive the messages encoded in light form from different realms without necessarily seeing the entire vision.

We call it channeling the Sacred because through such art you now have the ability to blend with us and to bend your consciousness around the corner of three-dimensional living into infinitely higher and subtler dimensions. But don't get too preoccupied with light packets, frequencies, or vibrations. All along you've been making good use of them. Instead, return to your inner knowing and recognize that you already carry within you the most vital part of channeled experience—which is that you share with all Light Beings a fundamental energetic core resonating with the core of others, and, in fact, you are a Being of Light.

Chapter Six

Diving into Diverse Channeled Experiences

The Guides Speak:

It's All About Relationship

After all is said and done, channeling is really no different from any other process of being with someone, striking up a conversation, or getting to know someone well. It's all about relationship. You have had many relationships—past, present and future—and some have ended suddenly, some have lingered, and some have gone out like a long-burning candle wick. In the same way, new relationships are being formed minute-by-minute and your hunger to meet with Divine acquaintances matches these up with and for you.

Imagine you went to high school years ago and developed a close relationship with a friend who then moved to another country. Fifteen years later when she returned home, you realize that although time has passed your relationship is fundamentally the same. It hadn't changed at all, and the love that had been dormant is once again alive and well. Now take this thought a little farther out into time and space. Suppose that you had a relationship with Thoth or Isis, or with Mother Mary, Yeshua, or St. Germaine. In some other location, or at some other time, you beheld their presence, practiced their teachings, or simply accompanied them on their journey. The soul remembers these connections, although they may not be currently available to you. Yet the memory is stored within, and when there's a true need for connection, we hear you cry out. We would expand upon the old adage, "When the student is ready, the teacher appears" to say, "When your soul hungers for deeper connection, those Divine relationships re-surface." It's a longer version of the saying, but you get the idea.

If you recognize that in fact you have a relationship with EVERYTHING, then this becomes a fertile field for exploration. You have relationships with family, friends, co-workers, neighbors, teachers, students, postal workers, store clerks, gardeners, and grocery store managers. Some folks postulate that there are roughly 10,000 people whom you know or influence in one way or another. However, that's still too limiting.

You have a relationship, as we said, with EVERYTHING. That means the flowers in your garden. That means your donkey, your dog, your bicycle, and your car. That means your cat and your chrysanthemum. You're related to the waterway, the tree you hug, the hill you climb, and the path you choose to follow. All your gifts and talents—in a sense, are related to you, just as you're related to them through your creation. If you take this a bit further, then everything you've created or brought forth in this lifetime now has an independent existence. Think of it. The words that comprised your Ph.D. dissertation now stand on their own. The business report that shifted how you worked as a team. The plans for a beautiful new garden—as well as the beautiful garden itself—all stand on their own. The podcast, the blog, the poem, and the pastry—everything has your stamp—or what we call your Signature Energy.

Your relationships are infinite and eternal, stretching in all directions. Therefore, channeling is a most excellent device to bring you into contact—not only with others whom you've known and loved—but also with multiple dimensions and multiple creations you've brought forth. When you grasp the potential that channeling has to offer, there's an extraordinary opening to derive information, inspiration, challenge, relief, validation, and re-visioning of all that is part of your life. For nothing is static; in fact, everything you've touched continues to unfold and evolve in the same way that you yourself evolve in continual and uninterrupted motion.

Dr. Jan Seward, Ph.D.

Metaphysics, Astrology, and Channeling Work

Dr. Jan Seward is a clinical psychologist, astrologer, and sound and energy healer who has worked in the integrative healing arts space for almost 40 years. Dr. Jan, as she is known, brings a spiritual dimension to the world of everyday practice and is dedicated to helping people realize their true, Divine nature. Working both privately and as a clinical professor of integrative medicine and as a metaphysical and life management practitioner at a major health and wellness resort, Dr. Jan has shared her gifts and wisdom with people of all ages and walks of life. She is blessed to live in a community that celebrates spiritual wisdom and connection. You can learn more about her at www.drjanseward.com.

Dr. Jan speaks:

The way that I would describe myself in terms of channeling would be as someone who is claircognizant. I don't generally hear or see things. I probably feel things; however, when information comes through, it comes through as perceived fact. It arrives spontaneously, and I feel compelled to share it just as it is.

This channeling developed as a surprise. The first place I noticed this kind of channeling was in my psychotherapy practice. My training was in-depth psychoanalysis, and so a big part of that consisted of making interpretations. What would happen is that I would offer things to my patients, and they would say, "Oh my goodness, how did you know that?" Or "How can that be?" I would have pre-cognizant dreams before I met with them, and the messages that came through often resonated with great impact. Now, this is not uncommon in the psychoanalytic field. I was not trained as a Jungian analyst, which is interesting, because this is their métier. This is their bread and butter.

But I was trained as a Freudian analyst, and although this type of approach is less common for Freud and for Freud's followers, Freud himself explored the link between clairvoyance and psychoanalysis. Most people don't realize that the cultural milieu that Freud traveled in was heavily into spiritualism and psychic phenomena. Freud studied with Pierre Janet who was using energy and hypnosis. So like Freud, my roots also come from this field of energy and spirituality. And of course, Freud's *Interpretation of Dreams* was a seminal work. The entire introduction was an encyclopedic survey of dream work from the time of the Egyptians to the present! It was through Freud that I was first introduced to the great Egyptian practitioners and dream-workers. And I love that story about Freud and Jung, who while delving into the world of Spirit had to stop when a cabinet exploded in Jung's office!

There was really no precedent in my family or ancestry for channeling— no channelers or card readers or healers. It wasn't until I was 39 years old that I even had my first astrology reading. It happened after my first husband had become ill and wanted to explore through some type of psychic mediumship whether he'd live or die. He had dabbled in esoteric Judaism and so we met with a man who, though he was an astrologer, was also a gifted channel: so prescient, so targeted. Besides working with my husband, he was able to see things in my life that had profound impact for me. This opened me to the use of astrology as divination.

After that I began doing research on my own. Discovering what being claircognizant meant was very difficult; however, I was able to validate it through research. After my husband died, I had some visitations, a little poltergeist, if you can imagine. In addition, I met Patricia, an amazing channel. Also, I have a watery astrological chart (lots of planets in Water signs) and it signaled to me that I had some gifts to apply in this area. People with a predominance of Pisces or Scorpio (I have 5 planets in Pisces!), tend to be able to travel between worlds. In the rich tradition of divination, I found a home of sorts—after all we've had channelers from the Egyptian dream interpreters to the Delphic Oracles all the way to Nostradamus and today's Oracles. I also learned that there are two types of practitioners who travel between these worlds — those who have visions and dreams as a direct transmission, called Oracles (or prophets) and those, like myself, who work with objects, symbols, charts, or other divinatory methods. We're called "Technicians of the Sacred".

It was surprising for me to discover that that's my sweet spot. After channeling thousands of sessions for clients in therapy for more than twenty years, I applied and was accepted as a metaphysical practitioner at Canyon Ranch just three years ago. I felt very grounded in my practice, particularly using astrology for divination. As I began the work, however, I would feel or see members of the client's family, both alive and in spirit, coming in and offering messages. Then I was asked to add on clairvoyant sessions, which was edgy for me at first, but then I began pulling information from the ether, so to speak. When I made that leap, I dropped into another space altogether. It's hard to describe what it's like to channel in that way. It has nothing to do with your frontal lobes. Instead it is information that's passed on to you and it's up to you to let it in without question and share accordingly. Sometimes I would sit and write down simple words as they occurred to me before meeting with a new client. One time I remember writing down the word *desert,* followed by *cherry blossoms*. I couldn't imagine how these two images could go together, but when the client came in and sat down, I mentioned these things she exclaimed, "Well, that makes perfect sense! I was born in Santa Fe and then my family moved to Korea, where everything's in bloom..."

Sometimes when channeling I feel a certain pressure in the thoracic area, and I know that important information is coming through for the client. I've learned to let go of the need to edit, censor, or question the results. Instead, I work to maintain neutral space, functioning more as the conduit or container for conveying important guidance. Meanwhile, I'm enjoying the process of developing relationships with a host of different Guides. When I studied Doreen Virtue's cards, I met many Ascended Masters. I learned who Thoth was in a past life regression, in which I experienced myself as none other than Thoth himself. I felt that I had a man's body, the depth and wisdom of his mastery, and could see myself giving counsel to the pharaohs of Egypt. Quite a surprise! However, I've also had visitations from beautiful soft feminine equivalents, such as Mother Mary and Kuan Yin.

In this newly arriving Aquarian Age, you will see much more guidance and connections of a channeled nature since we've entered into a long period where air signs rule. Also, Jupiter, who rules Pisces and Sagittarius, is in the 9th House, which is where Spirit comes to join us. Uranus helps break down walls, and, along with Pluto's influence, we'll witness old rotted structures tumbling down. What everything is pointing to is that we must be our own best connectors and look for more pure light and accept higher vibrations coming in. Children coming in now are already attuned to these dimensions; they have more fluidity, openness, permeability and ease with things of a spiritual nature. The downside, however, has to do with potential addictive qualities or deceptiveness that they may develop. But in this very moment, as we're speaking with six planets retrograde in Gemini (June 2020), there is extraordinary potential for gaining clarity and insight. Traditionally, Gemini was one to wear masks or at times be two-faced. But now we have new options to choose: honesty, transparency and equality, plus the willingness to remove the old masks we used to wear but no longer need.

I, too, find my channeling practice changing and evolving. I use a spirit board to help elicit information, and now in a funny way I hear my Guides *kvetching,* "Do we really need to spell out these letters for you?" Everything is available if I tune in. So, I'm learning to get off the board and go into the void—or what we call the vortex. In every session I'm committed to holding the light, being a beacon, and feeling the light enter my body and then move out as it lights up the inner world and the consciousness of my clients. But it doesn't stop there. You can imagine this process multiplying and moving in all directions—like a bright halo around the earth—bringing light, awareness, and peace, and as this new age progresses, we can envision *everyone* winding up on the receiving end of Divine wisdom.

Jo Ann speaks:

I am delighted to hear the variety of ways in which channeled information can come through from the Divine. I sometimes think that our Guides are quite sneaky, making use of whatever gifts, graces, or even cracks in our armor that are there to provide an opening for their transmissions. It's also a great relief to feel help pouring through from the unseen—especially in areas where we don't feel so competent or at ease, as in the anecdote that follows.

What Business Is This of Yours?

Jo Ann's channeled sequence

When our author first realized that her genius lay in writing or scribing, but not in the world of business or commerce—she finally relented and engaged the art of channeling to help change her point of view. Jo Ann recognized that with the completion of her seventh book that she had indirectly launched a new type of business—not your ordinary model but still an endeavor that in time could enter the world stage. And yet within herself she noticed many ripples of resistance and pushback from within herself as she channeled different conversations. While new ideas and images popped up, at the same time, it was clear that certain obstacles needed to be released. Here we reproduce a portion of that interaction.

The Guides speak:

Jo Ann, we know you are averse to business and planning for a business—that's not how you see yourself. The heart of a business is creating something amazing and then selling what has value in other people's lives. But you got stuck in the selling part. For you, all that's good is always free. So, we ask you to reconsider sales and exchange as Spiritual practice. This is a good time to release the overlays that hold you back.

Jo Ann speaks:

I can't sell something that's not mine to sell! It belongs to everyone. This is universal knowledge. It's ancient; it's also modern. How could I charge for it? It's like being a hooker! If you were to ask me to sell my body (of work), then you pretty well know my body is not for sale. Not my body incarnate and not my light body. Truth be told, I hate marketing, sales, net proceeds, numbers, social media, target audience, Twitter, Facebook, and anything that can't be performed with a simple pen and paper. I am fine with the spiritual law that "like attracts like" but I have some walls up or some kind of hex around this idea that in order to launch my books, I must begin selling.

The Guides speak:

Then we would ask you this one question: what if you never came across Danielle's book, *The Council of Light*? We know you'd be devastated since that book changed your life. Our second question is, what if one of your works has the same impact in someone else's life? Wouldn't you want to make sure to reach that soul? So now focus on the overall impact and take your eyes off the transaction. Continuing in this vein, let's get creative with this process. What is it we're really trying to do here, when push comes to shove? We're simply reaching out. We've put out a searchlight and a big welcome sign. It's not a sale; it's an announcement. Change your vocabulary.

If your first child were just now born, you'd send out sweet little baby-faced post cards to friends and family. But now we want you to see that your friends and family extend out to the four corners of the earth and onward and upward into higher dimensions. If you merely send out a batch of postcards, you won't be reaching us all. We need more effective channeling to illuminate Divinity!

Souls are lining up so that Divinity can be reflected to them in a new and different way! They're eager and waiting to partake of and interact with Spirit, and to come to know themselves in the same light as that Divinity they're used to worshiping outside themselves. Would you hold back based on some old myth of Separation Consciousness that you must sell yourself? Now is the time for real outreach—out of your hands and into their hearts!

Channeling your Business

The Guides speak:

Now, Dear Ones, take this kind of channeled scenario and see how it might apply in your own experience. Although the relationship that you have with the world of business may be significantly different, the process of making connection, however, is amazingly the same. For example, it may be that you have a fledgling business you'd like to launch more fully. But you're not sure how to begin. Or perhaps you've had a start-up that just didn't *start up* as well as you'd like. Or the 40-year family business is engaged in inter-generational conflict and after all these years it may crash and burn. Or perhaps you'd like to move from one business model to another.

Whatever the state of your business—whether fully operational or just a thought-form — you can use the channeling process to get clear with all parts of it. Remember, you're in *relationship*, not just with the players, but also with every part of the process, animate, or inanimate—the environment, the product, the promotion, the business plan, the client, the customer, the culture—and so much more. What a beautiful opportunity you have to sit and rework everything to your satisfaction in this now moment. And so, we would like to point out without too much subtlety—that now is the time. In fact, this very 'now' moment provides the perfect springboard from which to begin your channeled investigation.

Kathi Pickett, MBA, RN, CHP

Energy Healing, Channeling, and Notes from the Guides

Kathi Pickett is an author, speaker, Certified Healing Touch Practitioner, Registered Nurse and wise, heartfelt channel for many beings. With her Master's degree in Business Administration, she became a director of clinical integration and later worked as manager of a community health center, where she introduced Reiki, labyrinth walking, and mindfulness meditation. She continues her channeled work and healing both at Canyon Ranch in the Berkshires and in private practice. Visit her online at: www.kathipickett.com

Kathi speaks:

I'm so happy to be here with you now, and I feel honored—even with this sense of being choked up—and with tears coming to the surface. It's not often I get to speak so openly about this channeling process, and it's not often people grasp how it comes from a such a deep and Sacred Space within. Invariably, words are not enough. It's a different universe we enter, and it's not always easy to describe. But folks who sign on for a channeled experience demand a lot: "Can't you sprinkle fairy dust on me and make someone suddenly appear?" They have unusual images of us as channels and sometimes difficult expectations of what we actually provide. Some think we can just look over our shoulder and point out which of their Ancestors has arrived for the session. Others think that channeling is as simple as turning on the spigot; water starts flowing and you can turn it on and off at will. However, it's not that simple.

My greatest gift is the welcoming I've given to Guides throughout my life and the sense of pure love and unconditional acceptance they've offered me. I'm also grateful for the ability to recognize the diversity and complexity of what comes through them. In addition, I deeply appreciate the gift of being able to return again and again into their beautiful presence. This work is sacred. It's working with light and the vibrations beyond light. Moving into that multi-dimensional space means moving into that place of perfection—of Oneness—of ease. There's no pain there. There's no sorrow, and neither is there joy. It's just space—as in vastness. It's wisdom. It's pure energy and often beyond any language we can evoke to describe it. If channeling has been the greatest gift in my life, then finding the means to communicate what I receive into the human realm is perhaps its greatest challenge.

But the presence of Guides and Ancestors is here and has always been available to us. Nowadays, I sense the aura of the Earth is expanding and so is the accompanying consciousness that goes with it. That means that Guides, Ancestors, and Angelic Presences are even more available to us than ever before. That's because there's less toxicity in the environment, less running around, and most importantly, less disruption in people's energy fields. As a result, when I work with people, things are coming up that are decades old. What is reported out is often a surprise, and people say to me things like, "I thought I had already worked this through," or "Why is this coming up now?" The more we enter the stillness, the more we are aware of the density in our energy field. We then realize that there is more to release. And the more we release, the more we fold back into the Oneness. I can hold space for others to enter that stillness and release other parts of the self that have been hidden. This is a good time to make a clean sweep.

What I discover, however, is that as people dive more deeply into this work and sense the presence of Guides and helpers, that their questions turn pragmatic: "Well, what am I supposed *to do* with that information?" Frequently they question, "What is the nature of my soul purpose?" They want clearer definition. It's funny how we humans always want to be saddled to form. What form can this take? How can I format it? When that comes up while channeling, I advise folks to release their resistance created around wanting a specific answer. The immediate work is to *remain* in the flow and not to *question* the flow!

For when you question the flow, you limit its qualities and can actually block the flow of energy and information that is coming through. I hold the space with neutrality; I don't expect any particular outcome, and when things come through I merely counsel folks to be curious. Explore! Learn more about this, for if you get curious about the message, then it brings more richness into your life and you're better able to fully experience the energy and spaciousness of the Guides and their knowing.

Detachment is the key. The more detached you are from any particular outcome, the more you receive deeper wisdom. Above all, I advise my clients to trust their experience. And I advise them to trust it as it comes through in this moment—whatever it is—and only in this moment is it true because the nature of consciousness is that it's constantly changing and evolving. It's like if you read through to the last chapter of this book, then you might say to yourself, "Good. It's over. I can move on." But it's not over. Your truth is constantly expanding and the information coming to you from all parts of the Universe—from Guides and *devas* and Angelic Beings—is also changing with you. And there's always more. So, in a sense, there's no end to this book or its applications, even though, of course, the pages do come to an end.

When I do channeled work with people, I often see a hologram of their energy in my mind. So, I may have an older person sitting in front of me; however, I can see them as a child, as a young adult or even in different form, or as an archetype. I never attach to just one vision of who they are because I recognize the multiplicity of forms and experiences that we all have taken as we cycle through different life experiences. It's interesting to me what people hope to experience during a session. Generally, they're hoping to make contact—that is, to connect with those who've died and passed on. Other times, they're hoping to derive a deeper sense of what propelled them into life and what constituted their soul contracts—the agreements they signed onto before incarnating on earth.

As far as my own Guides are concerned, they are multiple and have held different functions throughout the years. When I was as young as four-years-old, I first saw my Guides as beautiful tall angels or Beings of Light. They were so loving and benevolent that I felt very safe and always loved and protected by them; I never felt alone. Through the years I have worked with different entities; some remain, some come through at different times. I don't try to ask for specific beings or personages, although in healing work I may call upon Archangel Raphael, the one who deals most with healing arts. However, I just focus on the individual in front of me and ask for help with whatever they're presenting (or grappling with).

At different times I've been made aware of concrete Guides who present themselves to me with specific tasks or purposes. In my book *On Becoming You* (Balboa Press, 2018), I speak about Red Cloud, who came through in a vigorous and assertive fashion to remind me of my lifetimes as a Lakota and to replace the term "Native American" with *indigenous* people. After all, we were not American in any sense of the word. Red Cloud's energy is available to all—not just to me—because we happen to be related through a physical lifetime. Yet, since he was my father, I feel threads connecting my spirit to his, almost like silver ethereal threads that run down the ancestral lineage from him to me and back again. I have also felt lifetimes in the company of Ra, the Ancient Egyptian Sun God, and can witness the great healing and light brought in from those ancient dynasties. Even to this day, I feel a great affinity and healing presence in sunlight. I was strongly influenced by lifetimes spent in Egypt in multiple healings, soul retrievals, and in-depth sacred trainings that occurred there. Often, I recall the presence of a totem animal protecting me on a spirit level—a beautiful black and gray leopard. She first came through as a kitten (I suppose not to alarm me), but I realized that for a priestess in Ancient Egypt, the leopard would protect me from low energies and keep my energy field clear for the work I was doing. She has a similar role in this now moment. Only that lovely cat is out chasing mice and moles off of my *field* (that is, of course, my energy field and not the backyard garden).

When I started doing more energy work and completed the Healing Touch training, I began to sense different energies moving in and Guides who were more versed in the healing arts, so there was a shift from Guides who focused on me and my welfare to focusing on the people who came in need of healing themselves.

As soon as Jo Ann and I started talking, I felt both of us surrounded by Guides, and a host of friendly Spirit Helpers who are interested in this work. Their message was simple yet direct. And although this came through in relation to the work that you're reading, it is actually meant to encompass the notion of work from a broader perspective. So, as you read, notice what parts of this guidance resonate with aspects of your own life.

The Guides feel that the overarching theme of the kind of work that you have to offer has to do with the heart center. Everything you're doing comes from within. It comes from the Sacred Space surrounding and within you. Your heart is full, and your heart is healed. You can let go of any worries you may have had or fears or anything troubling you because in that Sacred Space, they no longer exist. When you come back into the Oneness, then you remember who it is that you are. You see the clarity of your vision. You feel the Wholeness, the fullness, within and around you. Your work and any of the other ways that you reach out in the world compose a big huge heart. Everyone's work eventually boils down to that heart-open space. It's all about learning to love oneself. And of course, this is no new message. It comes in many varieties and many different forms as we have the need to take in and accept its meaning at deeper and deeper levels.

We find ourselves pumping more light, more energy into your heart space; feel it expanding and reaching out in all directions. Loving yourself fully—having compassion and understanding for oneself—is the key that turns the lock for all other endeavors. It is the means by which Oneness is finally attained. When we are at one within ourselves, we are at one with all beings, and anything that does not conform is dissolved back in the Wholeness, back in the Oneness. That is the Source of life and breath for us all. So, for all of us, this is the time to renew our acquaintance with our own Inner being, our Source of love and light within. The sacred art of channeling reminds us we are never alone—we are seen, cared for and accompanied on this journey of life, bringing the very best of who we are out into the open—both for the benefit of others and especially for the benefit of ourselves.

Chapter Seven

Release Obstacles, Overcome Painful Patterns, and Shine Your Light!

The Guides speak:

Physicists have the best shorthand to describe the world of vibration. When you're in pure, positive energy, you're in *flow*. Whenever there's struggle or a diminished vibration, you're in resistance. Resistance consists of whatever it is that obstructs flow.

When in flow, nothing stops you. Vibrating at the highest frequencies, you build momentum and that momentum takes you anywhere, anytime. But when mind enters in, then pushback happens. By saying, "No, I don't want, I can't, I won't, I hate, not for me, no one ever, not now, it's not possible, no", whatever negation you invoke creates an obstacle and slows vibration. It alters your free flow in the world and when you slow down vibrationally, doubt, fear, anxiety, anger, resentment, grief, or any other kind of negative thoughts disturb your energy field. At any moment, however, you have the choice to observe your pushback and release its charge by fully locating and accepting its cause. However, when you bypass the source of your discontent, in a certain way you are giving it permission to remain in your energy field and further the effects of its negation. That may point to mental, emotional, or deeper physical disturbance, and eventually disease—all of which result from the slowing down of your natural vibration.

Working with Slower Vibrations: A Thoth Transmission

Channeled by Danielle Rama Hoffman

Danielle is an international coach and channel, keeper of the Ascended Master lineage of Thoth, and creator of Divine Transmissions, a powerful center for training Light Workers. For more complete and thorough information about Danielle, please see her full introduction in Chapter 12.

Thoth speaks:

Imagine slower vibrations are like drops of food coloring. Put a few drops of food coloring into a tiny vessel like a thimble full of water, the color quickly saturates the clear liquid. That's how slower energies show up in the old paradigm. They can grip you completely. Now, drop the same amount of food coloring into the ocean. The hue would barely be detectable. This is exactly what happens to slower energies when you shift from the old paradigm of limited consciousness into an expanded, multidimensional consciousness. They're still there but barely noticeable.

When you are operating from your true multidimensional nature, from your Divine Wholeness, you move through slower energies with ease. They show up, but they don't take you off course. You easily find your way back to your full brilliance and the next step on your journey.

Light Workers and Shamans

Jo Ann speaks:

Dear Ones, as we move through each chapter familiarizing ourselves with the different kinds of channeled work available today, continue attuning to your own internal process and to any call that may surface around engaging this ancient art of channeling. As you read on, you may uncover a facet of your own shamanic nature reflected through this process. You do not need to wear a strange costume, play a drum, chant, or dance around a fire in ecstatic trance in order to do the transformational work shamans do. Anyone can be a shaman. In fact, there are multiple shamans at work today around the planet, each in their own way discovering keys to unlocking slower energy patterns and helping you relax, release, and re-align with the Oneness and the Wholeness of your Divine connection to Source.

In the work of Marty Benjamin that follows, you can observe the multiple ways that he has learned to engage and align energy, thus helping promote true healing. Being in his presence has the sanctity of being with a shaman. And in truth, all whom you meet within this work are shamans, healers, and channels. They shine the light of the highest frequencies to help dispel the remnants of darkness within you. And they reach out from the position of Wholeness and Oneness, thereby restoring that same recognition and alignment within those whom they help align and heal.

Marty Benjamin, Ac

Combining Acupuncture, Energy Work, and New Modalities for Healing

Marty Benjamin is a licensed acupuncturist trained at the American College of Traditional Chinese Medicine in San Francisco, whose work is an eclectic mix of orthopedic acupuncture, field theory, applied kinesiology, body-centered energy work, the chakra system and channeled experience combining P-DTR and Voila, pain management and principles of the *Course in Miracles.* He divides his time between his private practice in Northampton, MA and his work at Canyon Ranch in the Berkshires.

Marty speaks:

There's so much to dive into in terms of the kind of work I'm doing now, combining acupuncture practice with work in Spirit—for example, using principles from the *Course in Miracles* and then adding in the newfound experience of treating clients hands-off while working online. That's brand new. There is a whole different way that I use my hands and my body to help focus my intention for healing. In each healing session that I perform there may be several layers that we move through in order to bring about alignment and balance.

The first thing that I do in preparing for a healing session is to center myself in truth. If it is really truth, then it exists for all of us. When speaking to a client, for example, that truth proclaims that I see you in your Wholeness. I don't see you as broken, nor do I see you as needing to be fixed. Instead, I look at imbalances that may be present, knowing, however, that the imbalances are part of the whole. I see you as whole, and I know that the essential you always has been, always is, and always will be whole. Yet, our ego-self or that part that is self-identified, takes on the illusion that we're somehow broken. So, my work involves holding the space for you to come back to the reality and the clear inner knowing that you're whole. That's the basic premise of all that I do. (Nothing real can be threatened nothing unreal exists). It may be difficult to understand, but the essential you can never be harmed. Anything that is perceived to be occurring as harm is not really real. Paraphrasing such key concepts as you find in the *Course in Miracles,* these are the essential truths that I work with.

If you're on the table, I can test your strength, I can test endurance, I can test the relationships between one part of your body and another part of your body. It's hard for me to test those things now, working virtually. However, I've been discovering as I work online that there is still great healing to be done. In fact, new resources from Spirit are gradually making their entrance. First of all, I can see you in your Wholeness. And I can open myself to what I call Source, or God. Pausing to come present to the energetics facing me, or what stands out as I assess you, I become an open vessel to assist in whatever needs balancing or alignment. Source is not something I can describe, but it's something that I feel; I feel what I'm part of and where I come from when I'm not isolated. It's nature and it's beyond nature. It is God.

Eighteen years ago, when I started giving lectures at Canyon Ranch in Lenox, I was terrified of public speaking. I had no issue providing acupuncture or pain relief sessions, but to actually face a group of people (and lecture) was overwhelming. Part of the reason I took the job at Canyon Ranch was because I knew it would force me to have to speak before an audience. So now, thousands of lectures later, I'm not terrified at all of public speaking. Very quickly I learned something that was essential to my work. When I'm walking toward the room where I'm giving a lecture, I invoke Spirit. And I say, "Spirit, I'm going to speak to this group of people. Please guide my words. Be with me and help me see what it is that they need to hear. Speak through me so that I can be of service to them."

When I finally enter the room and begin to speak, it's not the old me who shows up—who's self-watching, self-critical, and getting all panicky and afraid. You could say instead that it's the new me. I'm here to speak; it's my way of offering service, and I'm able to get out of the way. Then I actually have fun and enjoy being here. I learned this a long time ago, and now you could give me almost any topic to speak on, and I will invoke Spirit, arrive in the lecture room, and go to town. Although I channel things I'm familiar with, the truth is I don't always know what's going to happen. I don't plan for it; it just happens, and that's the same thing that occurs in my healing sessions.

When I first see a client, I usually have no idea what's going on with the person or what's going to happen in the session. But my first intention is always to meet you where you are and see you in your Wholeness. Even before that, however, I must take care of myself. Every day I use what I do with others to balance myself. I may sit for meditation or engage in different practices like Qi Gong or Tai Chi. In addition, I do the same work that I offer clients. First, I ask if I am emotionally balanced in this moment. If I'm not, then I find what's out of balance, and I work to bring it back into balance. If it's something in my physical body, I check in. I connect with my basic structure to see if I'm balanced sitting, standing, or lying down. If not, then I make the necessary corrections.

If the issue is emotional—perhaps I'm in conflict with someone in my family, then I look in a different direction. You can have stories in your body that are emotionally charged, that are part of your history, and if you start to focus on them, then you bring up those same feelings and vibrations and stir up things. There's always work to be done there. But as you sit here in front of me, or I sit facing you, I must ask the question, 'Are you present in this moment?' Are you balanced enough in this moment to be fully here and available? Or is there something so disturbing that you can't be present right now? If that's the case, before we do anything, we have to become present. So if I wake up in the morning feeling I have some angst in my relationship with my wife to work out, or if I'm nervous about my business, or worried about how I'm going to deal with my landlord, then I recognize that I'm not fully present and am in the grips of that particular emotional storm—whether it's mild or severe. So, however I work with myself, I need to get to a present state of being.

How to move through that storm? First, I sense what's going on. I recognize that I'm not calm and focused. Sometimes I'm aware of the source of disturbance; sometimes I'm not. Realizing that I need to talk to my subconscious, I have different forms that I use. One comes from the Emotional Code. It's a list of sixty different emotions that can take us out of balance like fear, jealousy, anger, panic, shock, terror, feeling unsupported, or feeling like you're taken for granted—all these kinds of things. So, I ask myself if what's out of balance is on the list, and I try to identify the particular emotion. Let's say what's thrown me off is feeling like I'm being taken for granted. Then that's what I work with.

However, returning to the core truth—that at all times I am whole and complete, if I'm feeling taken for granted, that thought pattern will take me out of my knowing that I'm whole. So, I ask myself what will bring me back to that centered place—to that inner knowing of Wholeness? I use the energetics of our chakra system and energy body because in a certain way, the chakras tell a story. Each chakra can point to what is out of balance in the body, which can be accessed through muscle testing. Usually what I find is that a key chakra is out of balance, and that becomes the priority to work with, while there is another in relationship to it that may also need attention. So, I balance the primary one using information from that as well as the secondary chakra to get in touch with the emotions. Using the example of feeling taken for granted, it might be the fourth chakra—the heart center—that's involved as well as the root, or first chakra.

The first chakra is all about security and support, survival and safety, so balance begins to return when I realize that what I really want is to feel supported in what I'm doing. And I can't get that from others. Real balance comes from inside me. So even though feeling taken for granted may be a projection involving others—what balances me is acknowledging that I have what I need; I'm whole and complete, and I am fully capable both of connecting with and experiencing the kind of support that I need right here within myself.

All the information can be found within you. So, if you ask what is it that I'm channeling, it's really that I'm helping you bring forth your story. Whether conscious or unconscious, it's all within you. So, let's say I'm working with someone and we discover that the second chakra is out of balance. Then we learn that it has to do with relationship. So, the next question is what is the issue? Who is involved? Is it someone in your family? If it is, find out who it is —your children, your aunt, your mom or dad—and explore where the disturbance comes from. Gradually you pull out a story. Oh, it's about your mom. Then you go up to the third chakra, which is about confidence, power or strength. So, you ask what aspect needs to be recognized there? Then you go into your heart, so in the case of feeling taken for granted—it might be self-acceptance or self-love or joy.

When I completely accept myself, then I can be in the presence of others, and whether they're attentive or not, I'm not pulled by the force of these feelings; I'm fully accepting myself. I don't have to react to their actions. Or it might be that it takes me out of my joy, and I need to re-connect with my joy. And all of a sudden, when I realize it, the disturbance goes away, just like a little breeze fluttering in the air. Whatever the emotion is, there's invariably some storyline connected to it. As I go through the chakra system, that story begins to emerge, and sometimes other stories attached to the original one shows up. So, it's an organic process. We'll find the source of the emotion. Then we'll find out what balances the panic or emotional distress, and joy and equanimity are restored.

Now, there are many layers on which my work continues. For instance, I may have someone with deep physical issues, trauma, or PTSD. In that case, I first want to create safety. They may feel unsafe in the world in general, but right here, in this moment I have to ask, "Right now in this room, are you safe with me?" If not, then we need to go through a process of finding out how to recognize safety. This might involve them finding someone else to work with. Or perhaps for a woman, working with a guy is threatening, and they need to find a woman practitioner.

So what I'll have them do is feel the energy of joy or the energy of peace (we might use instances from their past or even from their imagination)—whatever experience they want to restore within their being—and once there, I'll use a breathing technique to support and underline the process. So, the client will breathe in to the count of four and exhale to the count of eight on a steady rhythm. What happens when you're breathing in and out in this way is that you're loading your body with certain neurotransmitters that support feelings of safety and joy and that take you out of fight or flight. When you breathe in, you're loading the system with norepinephrine, which accentuates sympathetic dominance, but then by focusing on the exhale for a longer time, you're actually loading acetylcholine and restoring parasympathetic dominance (that part of the nervous system that promotes rest and digest), which creates feelings of great joy, relief or calm.

While focusing on those feelings of peace or safety, you combine this particular breathing technique that then helps anchor in those feelings and make them more steadfast and reliable. You're imprinting them into your system. After a short while, your body responds by sighing or yawning or swallowing, and at that point we know that your system has gone through a change—when you get that primitive reflex, something has shifted. So, when someone is in stress or PTSD, there are certain thought progressions that are trapped in their brains, like a feedback loop that they're unable to escape. Using this anchoring process, we're allowing that to change. We have interrupted that configuration so you're no longer locked into that compensation to your system. When you combine the chakra work with this deep breathing process, there's great opportunity to work with and release deep-seated trauma and emotions from the past.

I remember one man in particular, whom I saw a while ago. He had been suffering from what he called extreme anxiety for the past forty years. He then revealed to me that he had been a survivor of sexual abuse, both within his family and also within the clergy. Never at rest, he said this had totally shaped his life. In addition, he said that his entire purpose in life was to work. Although he has family, he can't even focus on them; all he can do is turn his attention to his work. If he succeeds in working continually, that becomes his only source of self-worth. Through the tools that I've alluded to, we were able to go into his past. He was open enough at that point to allow me to help access his story. Our stories are all there—but often deeply submerged in the case of trauma or PTSD. Through our joint process I was able to help him encounter things he had never told anyone before, but I simply read his book, to put it bluntly.

We worked to have him go back into his past and reconnect with events and with himself in a loving way as a young boy. Not only did he have the abuse done to him but he also acted it out on others when he was younger, which created such a tight knot within him that he couldn't accept himself at all, even despite the fact that he had been victimized so many times earlier on. He was in terror all the time about what happened. So when we went back through events, we found out what he needed at that time in his life and what would help him come to recognition of his Wholeness, and then we invited that version of him at an early age to come forward and help his present self accommodate all that went on and restore balance. So, we went back and forth, and out of that he began to merge these different versions until his cycle of self-loathing and condemnation was transformed. Then he realized with great awe and joy that he could relate to and enjoy his children and hold them to his heart. And he could hold himself with compassion. In a period of a few months, his whole life had undergone change; he reconnected with his family, he started enjoying life, and he no longer needed to make work his sole ambition or center of his existence. He still works, but it has a much different emphasis than ever before. He now finds his worthiness from within.

Many people, including Bonnie Cohen and the methodology of body-mind centering, influence the work I do. Of course, it developed through studies in acupuncture school at the American College of Traditional Chinese Medicine in San Francisco, and through post-acupuncture school studies. After acupuncture school I continued studying; since I was always getting physically hurt, I was interested in learning how to get out of pain. I needed to know how to get my body working again, and to learn how to get movements working and not feel restricted in any way. I studied all that I could, especially concerning orthopedic acupuncture and pain. And then, I studied Orthobiotomy; something called Pain Neutralization Techniques and P-DTR (Proprioceptive Deep Tendon Reflex), which is the work of Dr. Jose Palomar, (the Voila method). There are also many other applications based in kinesiology and transformational work that I've learned. It's been a very organic and multi-faceted development.

Many years ago, on the recommendation of two former acupuncturists from Canyon Ranch, I went and studied the neuro-modulation technique with Joseph Feinberg. He used muscle testing and varied types of inquiry to delve into someone's system and create balance and healing. At the time I found that I was unable to do muscle testing. But later when I was engaged doing orthopedic work, testing the action of the psoas or the anchoring of the quadriceps muscles, for example, I gave another shot to that type of muscle testing and instead of getting garbage, I got absolute clarity. So, I was able to move on and use testing on my own body as well as surrogate testing to see what was happening in another person's body.

I had a gentleman I was working with who had a case of acute Achilles tendonitis. A handful of sessions in, I realized that he was completely unable to curl his toes on either foot. And if he tried to curl his toes, his feet would spasm. So, we did all sorts of physical interventions and got things to start to improve, but there was an emotion trapped in his low back/sacrum. Investigating further, we learned, sure enough, that when he was a young boy, he jumped off a roof but missed the tree he was aiming for and instead landed on his tailbone. At that time, he was sure his life was over, or that he was going to be paralyzed from the waist down. The emotions related to that experience got trapped in his system; however, when he felt empowered to go back, he was able to connect with the emotions and move toward what he wanted and come back into his Wholeness. He went from thirteen or fourteen years of not being able to curl his toes at all to being able to curl his toes easily. It happened in seconds. As soon as he cleared the emotion, the pathways were open. But that's what happens in every session—it's not necessarily as extraordinary as in this example—but once we access the underlying issue or story, there's an amazing speed by which a person recovers function and a sense of peace and groundedness.

I've learned that it's important when I'm doing this work to remain in balance because otherwise, I'm going to be projecting my imbalances onto the client and not working from a place of clarity or peace. The truth is that every single person I work with is a gift to me because I get to deepen and to unravel my story. Everyone who comes is a gift, and sometimes my work is allowing the client to be fully present, while allowing myself to be fully present and then discovering—much to my amazement—how the gift is right here in front of me and invariably turns out to be a Source of connection, grace, and joy.

JoAnn speaks:

Despite years of having offered counseling and energy healing, it still amazes me to discover how much can be stored within our bodies. As healers, most of our work consists in teasing out the "code," or association between symptom and story. But in truth, we have not even come *close* to exploring the full ramifications of the Body-Mind-Spirit connection. At times channeling work mirrors issues that we ourselves have struggled with; at other times channeling can surprise us by shedding light on long-forgotten baggage carried over from the past, as in Kathi's narrative that follows.

"I Don't Believe in Spirits"

By Kathi Pickett:

A 50-year-old woman came in to see me for a Healing Touch session. Once she was on the table and comfortably situated, I assessed her energy field. What we discovered was that her root chakra had been blocked due to lifelong feelings of abandonment that were carrying over now and affecting her relationship with her husband, whom she loves. That underlying sense of anxiety that she feels has kept her from expressing unconditional love.

During the session, her father presented himself to me in Spirit. He was adamant about letting her know she had never been abandoned. "I have always been near. I have watched over my daughter her whole life. Tell her that!" At that moment she stirred, opened her eyes and said she felt something. She asked me, "What is going on?" I said that

I sensed the presence of a Spirit and wondered if she did as well, since she seemed startled. She said, "No, I don't believe in Spirits."

Nevertheless, her deceased father kept on insisting that I tell her how much he loved her, how much he had always loved her, and that he had never left her in Spirit. So bravely I said, "Can I ask you something?" She agreed. "Who do you think pushed you out of the way of that lorry?" She sat straight up on the table and recounted to me that when she was in her early 20's living in London, she stepped out into the street and immediately felt as if someone was pushing her out of the way of a truck. That gesture saved her life. She added, "Then I looked around and there was no one there."

So, this dear woman started sobbing and realized that her dad had always been with her. I shared other times when he was present so that she would be sure. She told me that this information completely changed her life. She felt free, she felt loved, and at last—fully capable of loving her family as she had always wanted to do.

Sorting Out the Obstacles

Jo Ann speaks:

I relate strongly to that issue of abandonment. What started out as a review of the problems I've had with publishing turned into an uncovering of an old wound, not just from this lifetime but from multiple prior experiences. And that was the wound of abandonment—feeling as if I had been kicked to the roadside. For help with this, I am indebted to Thoth, who tells it like it is. I am also aware how Yeshua sends brilliant love-force energy and the Magdalene's surround me with their constant comforting presence and support. Oddly enough,

I also invited in Ganesh to this session; he's the sweet little boy with the elephant head, so revered in India, because he has the innate gift to help us release obstacles. And I knew I was standing in the midst of one mighty obstacle—that at the time felt more like a pit of despair.

It had to do with disseminating my work. To explain further, I felt an extreme sluggishness and lack of collaboration from my former publisher on the last three books that we had worked upon together. It was hard to get questions answered. I didn't understand the basis for much of their promotional work. It seemed as if their cookie-cutter approach completely bypassed the nature of my spiritual volumes and the targeted audience to whom they might appeal. Dismayed to learn that in the first two quarters of 2020, only 31 books of the *Twenty-first Century Gospel* had been sold, I felt myself quickly sinking into a place of despair, dissatisfaction, and resentment. All that money! All that time! All that effort! And it felt like no one really had my back. So once again the obstacle of the old abandonment ghost reared its head. I realized with a certain sadness that the greater obstacle was ME—at least temporarily. But the Guides didn't leave me guessing for long.

The Guides speak:

As your Guides, we wish to sort out this so-called obstacle you keep referring to, for in many ways it occurs as illusion. We would not diminish the experience of abandonment that you have had in several lifetimes, including this one. No doubt it has left certain impressions in your heart and mind—impressions we wish to reinforce are based on incomplete knowledge about yourself. We have never abandoned you. Nor have you been left to your own devices, although you experienced one lifetime where your mother left you and your father never showed up. Needless to say, there were others who picked up the thread and brought you wholeheartedly into their lives, but the sense of being left still remains with you in some fashion.

Now is the time to let it go. Now is the time to know that you are being fully taken in, taken up, and taken seriously. And above all, taken clearly into the arms of love. Your Council of Light continuously works with you, surrounding you with light, championing your work, and cradling you in our Divine love. We also wish to remind you of all those beings who love you and claim you as daughter, sister, aunt, friend, counselor, or beloved. Now is the time to remove your blinders and come present to the all-encompassing love that is your reality. Even as you give love to others so generously, we pour more love into your heart and more love. No one would suspect you feel any sense of abandonment because your love and care for others is so vital and strong that it buoys up their lives, their sense of wellbeing, and their soul-force.

We recognize that at times it may be difficult to let go of the old reality, perceived from the lens of Separation Consciousness; however, you have entered a new era and a new lifetime, even within the span of this one. You've crossed the threshold of separation into unity, into a new level of energy, frequency, and consciousness. Now you have the ability to see life for what it is. You have the ability to know yourself as pure Divinity: bathed in love, reclaimed in love, reframed in love—such that now you are nothing other than love itself. Remember how much you appreciated that saying: "The only remedy for love—is MORE love!" You are never abandoned; you have never left us, nor have we left you. If you search for our address, you'll find it easily. We live in a special district called LOVE—where we all dwell together in Oneness.

Chapter Eight

Wealth, Prosperity and the New Paradigm

Jo Ann speaks:

There is a well-known hymn in the Christian tradition that calls for a new vision. You may recognize the first two lines: "Be Thou my vision, O Lord of my heart; Not be all else to me save that Thou art..." Now this raises an interesting question. How can we place a righteous hymn in the middle of a chapter on wealth and abundance? Though indeed it seems strange to juxtapose a plea for a God-centered life with a bold discussion about wealth—nevertheless, there's a secret enclosed in this opening verse. You might call it a key that unlocks the new paradigm.

In the old paradigm, wealth is something to be obtained by trickery and corruption. There's a distinct line of demarcation between those who have and those who have not. In addition, having a significant amount of wealth implies something wrong or unrighteous about the owner. In the new paradigm, however, wealth is available to all. Wealth exists for the benefit of all. The old overlays about good and bad, or right and wrong, have gone into dormancy, and most importantly, everyone has equal opportunity for access, once the right key is turned in the lock. So, what exactly is that key? Again, it's hidden in the hymn mentioned earlier, which now brings to mind an old movie called *Jumpin' Jack Flash*. In that movie, the key to solving a crime is hidden within the Rolling Stones song. Once she's been clued in, Whoopi Goldberg, the heroine, madly searches through the words of the song, only to discover that the key is plainly in sight! But she has had to shift her search from the old to a new vantage point, discovering that the song itself is the *key*, and it's sung in B-flat!

With the new paradigm of wealth, there is also a key that unlocks untold wealth for everyone. It lies in those ten words, "Not be all else to me save that Thou art..." If we were able to unravel the mystery of God's presence and God's true nature, then we would truly understand there is no obstacle, no limit and no judgment regarding abundance. And there is no dictate that says you can have it only if you're deserving. The true Divinity that is our common heritage gives us access to great wealth, to great abundance in all realms, and to the ever-present and everlasting generosity inherent in Spirit. However, there's no longer a boundary between Spirit and the material world. What we need now is an enlargement of our vision to truly encompass what's Divinely available, what's ours to have, and what's on its way to us, if only we get ourselves out of the way.

Jo Ann recounts a moment of magic one summer morning:

Following a long meditation process, I started arguing with my Guides about how hard-hit I was feeling, having invested so much money in the publishing process. I began to realize that having money in the bank was important to me, not so much because I live a profligate life, but because having something stashed away gives me a feeling of being safe and anchored in this world. And it helps me feel that I can get on with the real business of living, doing what I know how to do best. Over and over the Guides reassured me that wealth was on its way to me. But I laughed in their absentee faces! Soon enough, however, I realized the joke was on me. At exactly 8:00 am that same morning, when I sat down checking emails, the first one that popped up was from my dear friend Liz, who, aware of my financial concerns, had just mailed me a check for one thousand dollars. She urged me to accept it without complaint because she was in a position to give. Could I possibly be in a position to receive? There's the rub!

That is the kind of request that's presented to each of us in this new paradigm. Can we open ourselves to receive more than ever before? And can we acknowledge that the God of the old hymns was more impoverished than the God of our brand-new vision?

Wealth Whisperer:

Soleah Dance

Soleah Dance is a Quantum Light Practitioner who is dedicated to helping people to recognize the light and the natural gifts they bring to all aspects of life. Soleah shares both her financial insights as well as the channeled messages she receives from her Guides, having developed these capacities during her work as a financial counselor. Her official title is Senior Retirement Plan Consultant. Most recently, however, Soleah has been developing communities of like-minded individuals in coherence with the Councils of Light, for the purpose of supporting each other while anchoring light onto the planet in potent ways. She sees her greater task is to help raise the vibration of humanity and direct frequencies towards the evolution of Unity Consciousness.

Soleah speaks:

We are solidly entrenched in a new paradigm now, in which channeling shows up more abundantly and yet can look any kind of way. I feel that there are aspects of the so-called new age paradigm that may actually create stumbling blocks for people, thinking that if the channeling doesn't happen a certain way, or if I don't know who it is that I'm talking to, then it's not working. And I'm not worthy to be expanding my light and taking this on. What I've seen are huge delays for Light Workers who have not yet become aware that they ARE Light Workers. A lot has to do with the fact that they're trying to find their way based on old stereotyped ideas of how things should be done.

Working with Different Channels and Light Beings

I've received a great deal from Micheila Sheldon, a full-on channel, who's incredibly gifted. She's also a perfect example of what I've been alluding to—she didn't even realize that she could channel until a series of events unfolded in her life, and now she works with all kinds of councils and Light Beings. Early on, I felt drawn to her methods and took every course she offered, as well as participating in what she calls her Inner Light Workers Circle. Later on, I became drawn to Danielle Rama Hoffman and her channeling of Thoth and other Light

Beings. I completed her Divine Light Activation course in France at the beginning of 2019 and then her Quantum Light Practitioner licensing program in 2020 and have become solidly placed on that path in my life journey. It feels like it happened eons ago—funny, how it seems like we're going at warp speed and at a snail's pace at the same time.

I met Danielle when I was working with Saryon, another channel who works with St. Germaine and many other Masters, and offers deep healing work—I had just completed his courses when he paired up with Danielle for Divine-to-Divine, an online program, and that's how I got to know and work with her. I absolutely adored Danielle's way of working with the Guides; she just cuts right to it. There's no chit-chat, no small talk. She just dives deep into the wisdom of her Guides, and all of a sudden, we're off to the races!

Right now, I feel like I'm gathering my own "family" of Light Beings, and the statues I've collected while traveling support me in that process. I have altars all over my Zen den where I do most of my work. There are sacred pieces on each of these five altars, which basically come alive for me every morning during my practice. I go around lighting candles; I greet everyone, thanking them for their presence, and gradually I feel myself attuning more and more to their different energy frequencies. Earlier on I never really understood what Danielle Rama Hoffman meant when she said a particular Light being was "moving more to the forefront of this Divine transmission." Now I get it. I can feel the different energetic presences emerging; yet everything feels spontaneous and unplanned. When I sit down, I don't say to myself, "Now I'm going to channel." I'm not a planner like that. I follow the energies. Without being attached to a particular outcome, I just wait to see what happens. It could be that I'll be sitting there and out of nowhere begin sobbing for no apparent reason, or I will actually begin speaking and a full-on channeled teaching comes through. I am aware that many times these are messages for my own self-healing.

I've also become more sensitized to the changing of frequencies. This happened the other day when Mary Magdalene came through. It's hard to explain, but I shift from the kind of egoic state where I'm the one presenting, to a different perspective where I actually start talking to myself on behalf of the Light being who's involved. Suddenly the energy in the room changes, and I feel very much at home conveying the idea or message. It's a very sweet feeling. So, first Mary Magdalene came through, and then she faded into the background, while Anna came through with an entirely different energy and a different message. I wish I had been recording, but at times these things happen spontaneously; as I said, I don't plan for this, though that may in fact change. But it's not always easy to do—especially when I'm out walking in the forest. It's amazing the kind of visitations that occur there.

The Many Possibilities for Channeling

I love how open the work is and how in effect there are billions of streams of possibilities, as Danielle herself mentions. Now there are so many different methodologies and types of channeling available to us that were never available before. In the Ancient Mystery Schools, Light Beings like Anna and Isis or the Hathors never had technologies we now take for granted—imagine knowing that tonight you'll be having a Zoom session with Mary Magdalene! But of course, the technologies that they did have were far advanced then and have further evolved today. As a matter of fact, in the last course that I took with Micheila, the focus was on the Divine Feminine and a variety of beings, including Mary Magdalene, Isis, Hathor, and Mother Mary came in describing their very personal experiences while they were here on the earth plane.

Each of them brought in several practices working with alignment through breath and the chakras.

When channeling, I don't see or hear words, but I feel things in my body. The changes in my body and the sense of vibrational resonance are most important, and I'm also beginning to move more into balance with the masculine/feminine energies; at first it was just Mary Magdalene coming through, and now I feel Yeshua in the background and present with her. So, my sense is that I will be working more personally with Yeshua, and I'm delighted with that. Part of my gift and my challenge is to bring the high-energy frequencies of this work into the lower density spaces of the corporate world. Channeling is a way to redirect energies caught up in the old paradigm structures of business, finance, and the material realm. For a long time, I wanted to get away from that altogether. However, I keep being brought back to work in the mainstream, and now that I've overcome a few internal hurdles, I recognize that it's okay to do so, and it's safe to bring all of who I am into whatever work I'm doing.

It's wonderful to see how in my work in the financial world, I have been developing the gift of channeling more and more. My official title is Senior Retirement Plan Consultant. I consult with the committees of various companies who are the fiduciaries, overseeing their company's retirement plan—usually their 401K plans, and I've been in this industry for more than 27 years. I also ran my own business with these same types of clients, but now it seems that the focus is shifting more toward the world of Spirit, eliciting messages not only about money, but also about living life in alignment with who you truly and authentically are.

It's amazing to witness the kind of transformation going on at my office; certain people have left who had a negative impact on the energy of the whole; and I've developed a little circle or posse of individuals who've expressed interest in realms beyond the third dimension; they're starting to have their own wake-up calls! Every morning we create a ritual together, and I do a card-pull to give them a read on the day's energetics. I love using Louise Hay's Positive Thought cards, which were gifted to me by one of my colleagues in this posse. After I pull a few cards, we have a group chat, and I may take pictures of the cards and send them to other members of that circle.

How the Guides Support Us

It's fascinating the role that various Guides have taken in helping us channel and develop deeper spiritual connection. Even though they were over-lighting these courses and teaching us various methodologies, these are just starting points for the new human who is here now. For, in fact, we are now energetically structured in a different way than the Guides were before, and so these tools can be adapted by us in our new and more accessible way of being. Our energetic patterns have shifted; so has our DNA. Channeling was very much a part of the Guides' awakening process, but they really want it to be known that we're to use them the way that our systems direct us to use them, in whatever way works for us, based on our evolved bodies, systems, and environments. It may very well morph into something completely different or something altogether new and unique.

Look at the tool of deep breathing. The breath in any form is probably the most powerful transmission of Divine light that we have to utilize, but how we do it, when we do it, and with what frequency we do it, as well as how we direct our awareness while doing it and what results within our being, that's all new. We're in a completely new world.

Accepting Leadership

Long ago, if people had told me that I would be channeling anything in the world of finance, I would have laughed in their face. However, more and more I'm stepping into a leadership role with this, and it's way different from anything I've ever done before. It's amazing to see what kind of an opening channeling creates; I'm freer and more personal both with members of my team and the clients themselves. As an example, I have a Zoom meeting with a client coming up, and I know that they're open to spiritual connection, so I'm also open to receiving more than just guidance about what to do with their retirement plan. It takes away the stodginess and rigid decorum of old-style corporate consulting, and we have a few laughs in the process! Often, I can feel it's simply silent but potent energy I'm channeling, opening up and holding the space in ways they may never know. This new type of encounter is energizing for everyone—we never know what will show up. I can joke with clients and bring in guidance—anything can happen, and the result is that we're having so much more fun in the process! This indeed is a big way that I've kept inspired in my current job, while exploring so much more outside of it.

Both with Saryon and Micheila, previous channels that I've worked with, I experienced multiple sessions where I was cracked open, blown away, and overwhelmed, trying to figure out what my work on this planet was all about. That can happen when you begin to realize there's much more going on than you ever thought, and that you yourself are so much more than you ever imagined. It's a continuous process to align with your true gifts and talents and find work in the world that's a match for both.

In fact, at this time in my professional life, many things have changed, and new directions are coming forth. In a manner of speaking, I've just entered the birthing chamber—if you can believe it—because right now I am giving birth to a totally new format and method of channeling. My guidance has been turned on for what I'm being prompted to do next. I'm still in the birth canal with it, but it's probably the boldest and scariest thing that I've ever done. I'm feeling the charge to create a new online presence for channeling. I will be bringing people together for a Zoom call and a group facilitation process similar to the one that has already been in motion (which is called, CALM, or Council of Awakened Love Masters). There will be similarities between the two endeavors; however, this new experience will be focused in a different way. We're looking to explore and experience ourselves in our highest light and at the same time to call in amazing prosperity and abundance, while also giving some of that back to the world. It's a brand-new wealth project that will help me deliver my legacy gifts from a whole different platform and I am delighted and lit up with the idea of combining things together that I love and can offer from my heart and soul.

So that's in essence what I'm moving toward. And I feel that I've been bobbing around for years trying to discern my mission around this. Now that I have this platform however, I am happy to facilitate our exploration of what true wealth is. While although it goes far beyond money, it acknowledges our need not only to attract but also to no longer be scared to desire money. Money is money. At its core, it's basically neutral, though it has a lot of negative overlays from our culture and conditioning. But if we recognize our need, acknowledge our worth, and choose to put it to good use, then money takes on a more balanced place in our lives and is seen as only one aspect that constitutes true wealth and abundance for us all.

The Guides speak:

Wealth Meditation

At any point that you're feeling less than or needing more than you currently have, this would be a great time to stop, push the pause button, and recalibrate: to change the predominant thought forms you may have been cultivating around wealth! As we mentioned earlier, wealth is fully here and fully available for those willing to accept it in this new paradigm. Contrary to old paradigm ideas about the virtue of poverty or scarcity, Yeshua proclaims the joy of generating more abundance. However, rather than living in poverty, the idea is to joyfully share this wealth with *everyone.*

What follows is a combined meditation and affirmation practice; you can set it up however it works best for you. But take advantage of this opportunity, if you choose, to allow your focus to broaden and your energies to expand into a refreshing new relationship with the incoming wealth and prosperity in your life.

After you've taken a few slow refreshing breaths, give yourself a moment to calm your mind and draw your senses inward. When you've come to a quiet place, let your thoughts move into a simple review process—or what we might call an "abundance inventory." Rather than focusing on lack—on what you've lost or failed to gather—instead take a moment to add up the balance of your life experiences that lean toward abundance. Consider health, family, friends, food, fun, or fortune—

whatever is currently present. Even in a difficult time, you still have friends or family. Or if you've lost a lover, you may harbor reasonably good health. If your bank account is dwindling, look at the abundance that shows up in other ways—in sunlight, breezes, fresh veggies, or whatever else may accumulate in your garden.

Now, step out of that frame for a moment, and consider any thought forms that may have tagged along, denying you your good fortune. Perhaps it's comparing what you have to others. Perhaps you only allow yourself a designated amount of wealth. Too much is un-spiritual. What about the poor people? Whatever the thought or conversation, let it reveal its cunning nature, and, if you choose, place it on the altar to be released. Let these un-prosperous thoughts simply disappear into the evening sky, while in exchange, you invite in a host of pleasing new possibilities.

Now take a moment to simply luxuriate in the awareness and feeling tone that you may associate with great wealth and abundance. Perhaps you travel to your heart's content now. Or you support worthy causes with great generosity of Spirit. Or consider building a spacious and beautiful home or sending your grandchildren to Europe. Let your mind wander over a broad territory of affluence, opulence, and joyful living that is completely guilt-free, available and on its way to you.

Then, consider writing some abundance affirmations. Create your own personal wealth mantras to resonate with who you are and what is calling to you to have now. They might sound something like, "I am free to receive everything my heart desires from the Universe. I enjoy having all that I desire. I enjoy spending or saving all that I desire." Or, "I accept, absorb, and accumulate wealth to my heart's content. From all that I personally receive, others also benefit. Wealth that comes easily and joyously to me circulates out to the world in all directions. I love having, giving, and receiving so much joy and abundance."

Finally, as you open this new wealth portal, take a seat and enjoy all that you have accumulated. What does it feel like to have your dreams come true? Can you find that thrilling place inside that resonates to prosperity? You have infinite capacity to receive what your heart desires and what lights you up. You just need to position yourself in the same vibrational place as that same wealth that is on its way to you. Imagine you can see the energies swirling around and beginning to take form. That is how your abundance unfolds. Sense how it feels to walk into that ecstatic place of receptivity. Here there is the glow of gold, there the shimmer of diamonds. How would you like your own wealth to be served up?

Chapter Nine

Uncover Your Divine Gifts

The Guides speak:

As you develop the skill of channeling, you may also begin to broaden your sense of who you are and what you're capable of. Part of that learning process has to do with distinguishing your gifts and talents—accepting the areas in which you excel—and the areas that are still under development. In the past, you may have had a limiting idea about yourself, such as I could never run a business; I could never craft a salad bowl or sew a designer dress. But in this chapter, you're encouraged to take a deeper look, perhaps remembering what it is that you already do and do well! And it may be that now is a good time to broaden your definition, gain clarity, and perhaps even uncover gifts of yours that haven't fully shown up on the radar screen.

Jo Ann Shares a Contrasting Experience of Gifts:

More than twenty years ago my then partner and I traveled to the Dominican Republic to visit friends of ours. We had been advised to stash our passports and extra cash in a safe place, so as not to worry while we traveled about. When we finally left for the airport in Puerto Plata, heading back to New York City; however, we realized we'd left our passports behind when we got to the terminal! They were stuffed inside a special flap we'd discovered behind one of the bureaus in our hotel room. So, we never made it home that day. (It's amazing how easy it is to hide things even from ourselves!)

However, that was not the case with my friend and extraordinary Intuition instructor, Ann Elliott. Her intuition saved her and her boyfriend from an expensive mistake. Ann recounted the experience during her Intuition Masterclass as an example of the benefits of being open to intuitive insights. While traveling in Europe one summer, Ann and her boyfriend were heading from Brussels to the Netherlands for a friend's wedding. Traffic leaving Brussels was untenable and the potential of being late was causing stress. A half hour into the drive, Ann started seeing an image of a hotel safe in her mind's eye. This made no logical sense, as she had not used the safe in the Brussels hotel.

As her partner drove the rental car toward the Netherlands, once again, Ann saw the exact same image of a hotel safe in her mind's eye. The image was clear and unmistakable. The third time the image appeared, Ann verbalized what she was spontaneously seeing to her partner. With a series of expletives, he pulled the rental car out of traffic and called the hotel in Brussels. Unbeknownst to Ann, he had left thousands of dollars in the hotel safe, forgetting to retrieve it after placing it there overnight. Miraculously, upon returning to the hotel, the safe was still locked with the money inside.

I relate these contrasting stories because it's so interesting what we remember and what we forget. It's also obvious that Ann has a special gift and a talent. Not all of us receive strong visual cues to help us navigate our personal journeys. But fortunately for Ann and her partner, they were able to recover the money he had left in the safe.

As I have come to know her, it's clear that Ann receives spontaneous flashes of insight; she has learned to use and trust intuition. As for me, well, there are other gifts and talents I can call upon.

In fact, for all of us, it's a good idea to take stock. We may discover things we've taken for granted or may not even recognize as part of our genius. Perhaps, we've been developing intellect, insight, or deeper knowing. Perhaps our compassion and loving-kindness have grown stronger. Sometimes our gifts are outspoken; sometimes they're soft and subtle, not even registering as a particular talent of ours.

The Process of Individuation

The Guides speak

When we first incarnate on earth and are tiny creatures, we continue to participate in and experience ourselves as one with the collective. Still undifferentiated, we rest contentedly in the great ocean of cosmic Oneness, lulled by the waves of our ancient connection. However, as we are nurtured and begin to grow into human form, little by little in our awareness, we come to recognize ourselves as different from the collective. The result: our individual selves begin showing up.

Besides the need to get to know ourselves as we are in our individual natures, we also come in with a very strong desire to grow and develop new skillsets, reaching into all areas of life for the sheer pleasure of learning and knowing. We want to know how things work. Jo Ann remembers when she first held her very young nephew in her arms and walked in front of the refrigerator. He pointed to the different magnets that were on the door, so she took one off and showed it to him. After he observed her efforts, he became engrossed in putting the magnet on and pulling it off the door, over and over again until it was clear that he had mastered the art of applying refrigerator magnets.

As each of us grows, we may become fascinated with the inner workings of an engine and how things combine under the hood of a car to make it run, or of how mixing certain ingredients together and placing them in a heated space provides a chemical reaction that creates the most perfect strawberry pie. We develop our gifts and talents out of this inherent drive—not only to know how things work—but also to be able to reproduce the results through our own efforts. So like Jo Ann's nephew, we go through life applying and taking down different magnets until they fully reveal their mystery.

What is actually being exercised is our inborn nature as Creator Beings. Think of an artist putting the final touches on a canvas. Before it was void and empty; now it sparkles with its own life force and design. Whether we are singing or writing or designing or building or mending or healing or planting or serving, no matter how we engage in life, we somehow find our way to duplicate the work of Creator and each in our own way bring forth new work—new connections—and ultimately, new life forms. To find our true work is to acknowledge our true gifts. To acknowledge our true gifts means simply to extrapolate from all our daily efforts that which brings the most joy and fulfillment.

If you've read through this far, then you've already tuned in to the extraordinary talents and abilities of the channels who have been sharing their work. It may take time before you can identify a specific gift or talent of yours that's been on the sidelines waiting for further development. In some ways that was Soleah's experience. Moving from within a corporate environment, she began to pull insights and inspiration from Spirit on behalf of those clients who were supervising 401K retirement funds. Likewise, after years of coaching Fortune 500 clients, CEO's, and leading entrepreneurs, Ann Elliott integrated her insights and intuition as part of the coaching process and in doing so, discovered that many clients were perfectly capable of receiving and acting upon the wisdom that came forth—regardless of its source.

Even when a gift is acknowledged and acted upon, there's always more to develop. Although Rev. Suzanne's knack for channeling came nearly forty years ago, she's spent many years refining the process and getting out of the way on more and more subtle levels. Opening to the idea of offering predictions would steer her work in a whole new direction! Earlier, Dr. Jan shared that she no longer needed to spell out every letter of every word upon receiving messages from Spirit. She could handle the *download* in one fell swoop! Clearly, one of her gifts is a great sense of humor and love of the absurd.

In her own words, here's how Dr. Jan describes her gifts:

My main gift is that I see you. Whoever I'm with—whether in a counseling or astrology session—I see you as you are. For some people that can be quite difficult. We don't necessarily see ourselves as the magnificent creatures that we are. I'm fortunate in my ability to see right to the heart of who you are, and that's because I was gifted with a mentor who saw me as I am and helped me do the same with others. I can see the breadth and depth of your Divine self and where your soul wants to go—because we are all on a path; we all want to go home. There's a certain call—a homing signal—that we may miss, we get lost or confused or the signal may be obscured by other voices or influences. However, that noise is not there for me in the same way;

in fact, I can't help but be overjoyed (and sometimes overwhelmed) by the magnificence of the person sitting in front of me. To know where that soul is striving to go is often shining through and just needs to be made conscious and affirmed out loud.

Naming our Gifts and Talents

Jo Ann speaks:

Gifts and talents can be approached in many different ways. You can call them your areas of expertise. However, that may in some cases sell you short. Having connected with Thoth and the Council of Light, I much prefer how they categorize our gifts and talents. First, there's the idea of working in your Zone of Genius—that which you do particularly well and in which clear creative flair is demonstrated. You may have attained that genius by working on it through many incarnations, like a child prodigy—a Mozart or a Beethoven. Anything you've been developing through time that now has power, refinement, and the stamp of excellence can be referred to as your Ascended Mastery. And those areas that you continue to develop and to master may in fact be what you offer the world as inheritance. They can then be referred to as Legacy Gifts or your Divine Legacy.

Right this moment is a good time to give thought to your special attributes. What contribution have you offered that you may have taken for granted in the past? What do you consider your Zone of Genius? What gifts or talents have you developed through the years? Conversely, which have been sidelined or lying dormant? And most important of all, what is now asking—no, crying out—for recognition and renewal? What strength or ability does the world need from you now? What gift gives back to you so many times when you are finally willing to offer it to others?

Jo Ann's Legacy Gift Speaks for Itself:

My gift is Spontaneous Creation, drawing on all kinds of wizardry and Magic, bringing in the humorous, the preposterous, the wise and witty and absurd, along with the knowing and the unknown joined together in a blessed and most unexpected Union. I am a consort and a cohort of the Divine. You could as easily call me Spontaneous Combustion as Spontaneous Creation for the two work well together, and I have so many luscious voices whispering from the Divine that it's a good thing I have more than a thousand ears with which to listen. I'm hearing stuff from all over the Galaxy. There's no use trying to sort it out by denominations, categories, catechisms, or continents. It's just zooming in. Is it the Man on the Moon? (No, cause she's actually a woman). Is it the yellow zinging rings around Saturn? Or are Mars men babbling? Everything that points to the unwinding, the unbinding, and the freeing up of precious Unity Consciousness—that's what lights up my work.

Jo Ann Responds to her Legacy Gift:

I love sharing the wealth of Creation with you. I love spreading the good news. So, if you're Spontaneous Combustion, then I'm the logs, the kindling, the spark, and Solar Flame that get you going. We're both *lit up*. I am truly amazed, deeply astonished, grateful, and reverential at the way that words, images and delight codes pour forth freely from us both, with help from our Light Being in Light Friends. Astonishing how little effort is required to shake up the universe! Now I ask you to combine energies with me so we can draw to us the perfect team to magnetize readers, students, and our finely matched customers —do you agree?

Legacy Gift responds:

Of course, of course, and if I were a horse, you'd be the carriage. We're traveling together and have already ramped up to warp speed, you didn't realize, for I'm a most galactic stead. I carry you through the stars but don't forget the seas. For you know I change form as readily as you breathe. Picture yourself descending, riding so effortlessly, on the crystalline saddle of your wee horse of the seas! We can circulate the globe and celebrate the news; even in this instant see how quickly Spirit moves—the word is out, the world awakes, yawns and stretches anew. Before your first ablutions, the Divine is onto you! So, you stir in milk and sugar to that morning cup of Joe, but this news creates such bubbles that from java, champagne flows!

Chapter Ten

The Magic of Creation

Jo Ann Encounters a Magic Butterfly!

The Guides speak:

Time and again we've been speaking about how artful you are in wielding magic and how throughout time you've been experimenting with supernatural creations. Yet you continue to question your own magical ability. And magic itself has gotten a bad rap through the ages. Consider this list we've compiled of the many ways that magic may be described:

- Paranormal event
- Sleight of hand
- Occult
- Witchcraft
- Miracle
- Voodoo
- Entertainment
- Illusion
- Deception
- Potion or spell
- Trick
- Disappearing act
- Reappearing act
- Unimaginable
- Extraordinary event
- Far beyond human experience

As you read through this list, notice that several definitions lean more to the dark side, or hold the idea of a con or a trick. So, consider whether your first thought of magic is of Harry Houdini escaping a tank of water or of Jesus turning water into wine? Some modern-day scientists explain that many events labeled as magic in bygone eras are now understood as reasonable effects of nature. In fact, explaining the source of such miracles (often known as debunking) now becomes the province of science. For example, Moses' ability to part the waters of the Red Sea so Israelis could escape Egyptian dominance has been revisited and reconfigured. Such an event that would have been considered scientifically impossible is now viewed differently. The explanation might be that if a cataclysmic eruption of a volcano in the middle of the ocean occurred during that epoch that it could easily have thrown a tsunami toward Egypt. That would have created such a vast disturbance that no doubt waters would have parted, leaving a real possibility for escape.

In a certain way you are parting waters every day in your own life. The reason you may neglect to call it magic has more to do with timing than with the actual outcome. In earthly terms it takes time, effort, and the transmuting of grapes and water into a new substance to create wine. But if you were to step out of your earthly timeframe, understanding that in fact all things exist simultaneously in this here and now moment, then there would be no need to wait for events to unfold. With your vision and magic alone, you would bring forth wine for the wedding or enough loaves and fishes to feed a crowd.

Well, that's just great, you say! Why didn't I know this before? Looking around, you have no validation of these effects; instead what shows up are markets collapsing, people hurting, wars, scarcity, illness, and a real lack of magic; none of which births the kind of empowerment that introduces a new construct a new reality. But when you come home to your original nature, then you recognize your constant participation in the Divine. This is not fancy rhetoric. It's actual fact. And in that participation magic happens continually, if not subtlety, moment by moment.

You have heard many channels and wise ones telling you that you are Creator Beings. Add to that the idea that you create worlds and then stretch your imagination a little further. It's ironic that your very magic is unknown to you and yet you continue to wield it in various ways. Consider the steps to take if you decide to build a boat. First of all, you've seen boats of all kinds, from canoes and kayaks to ocean liners. With many ideas to choose from, you map your vision, call in builders, or craft the boat yourself. But soon you're off sailing.

However, take the image back centuries to cultures where the native people had never seen a boat or encountered anyone crossing the water. Suddenly men arrive, but their boats are not witnessed until they actually touch down on dry land. Without a *concept* of boat or an *experience* of boat, the inhabitants could not actually *see* a boat landing. So, you can apply that to your own experience: you may not yet be able to *see* the kinds of miracles you create, but sooner or later the boat will show up in your consciousness and reveal its contents.

True magic is an alchemical process that all beings participate in and employ. From the boat example, you understand that having a vision of what you want is primary. Go back to our earlier discussion of the wingless bird. As a newborn creature with wings, you may have a vision that you'd like to fly. But you've never seen other birds flying. Now you have a choice; you can remain with that knowledge and stay on the ground, or you can begin to flap your wings and *imagine* what it's like. Soon you evoke the sensation of flying and can even picture yourself up on top of a tree.

As you sense the outcome, it approaches in your vision and then you feel it within your own precious wingspan. Against all odds and all evidence to the contrary (especially from birds who tell you it's never been done and you're stupid to try), you finally achieve liftoff. You're flying! That actually happens when you've achieved critical mass. We love the term critical mass because it deftly summarizes the transition from thought to physicality—a movement occurring from higher dimensions of thought into lesser and more dense experience, such as your three-dimensional reality. When at last you take note of your ability to create this special alchemy—in effect to move about, jump dimensions and procure the result of your thoughts, then you finally understand the true scientific nature of the magic that you create day by day by day.

The Magic in Your Life

Now, take a few minutes to pause and reflect on the magic in your own life. Although some of these concepts may seem far-fetched or not as relevant to your everyday living, relax and let go of any particular stance. You are magical! You are creating your very own brand of magic on a daily basis! But consider more deeply. Breathe, relax, and simply tune into the events of your life as they've unfolded. The magic you've created may not be self-evident, but upon closer examination you may discover your own artful gifts and talents. Sometimes magical appearances are so simple or subtle that they escape notice. Take the synchronicity of Jo Ann's penny pop-ups, as she calls them. Whenever there's a slight disconnect or she has the feeling that God has disappeared from her life, no matter where she is, a bright shiny penny invariably pops into view—generally on the ground in front of her within easy grasp. This has been going on for years (and we won't disclose the size of her penny collection at this point...)

There are many ways that your personal magic takes form. Although the instances outlined below are not intrinsically different from each other; nevertheless, they illustrate the many ways by which your Magical Self moves into action:

- **Synchronicities**: Someone you've been thinking about just called or sent a text.
- **Flashes of Insight**: Suddenly you know exactly where your pen, keys, glasses, checkbook, or phone are located. (Or your long-lost boyfriend...)
- **Weather Forecaster**: Something niggles at you before leaving for work and you grab the extra sweater, umbrella or raincoat— or, on the other hand, you're inspired to leave a little early and make it home just before the torrential downpour!
- **Déjà vu**: In this case something shows up you know you've witnessed before.
- **Intuitive Knowing:** You see through and beneath events to their core. Truth stands out in your mind. You may suddenly understand someone, what's caused a conflict or misunderstanding, or why you seem to react to things in a certain way. A light flows into your mind that penetrates the heart of life's conditions and experiences. And knowledge that once seemed inaccessible easily comes to you now of its own accord.
- **Greater Vision:** Your magic begins doubling, tripling, or quadrupling as you begin to grasp a new version of yourself in terms of work, family, geography, career, future opportunities,

or spiritual growth—and suddenly you find emails, ads, offers, requests, or other reminders pouring in that remind you how you've been sending out new versions of yourself into the universe! And, a whole new vision emerges! You begin to see the Divine connection between your view of yourself and what actually shows up in your life.

- **Deeper Connection:** That same connection grows and takes on more light, depth, and dimensionality. The vision of your possibilities expands exponentially; now you have a deeper appreciation for the magic that you are. Through prayer, meditation, or other forms of attunement, you are able to connect with Divine Energy and Wisdom at will.

- **Scribing and Channeling:** You now engage that inborn talent more deeply and more easily, freely bringing forth new wisdom, art, music, life forms, creativity, or messages from Guides, Spirit Helpers and Divine Beings. As you practice and gain proficiency, you soon arrive at the highest spiritual expression and now fully understand yourself as a:

- **Divine Creator Being:** Fully matched up with Light Beings in Light, and capable of entering into endless, effortless and amazingly inspired co-creation with the Divine.

Chapter Eleven

Unusual, Unpredictable or Just Plain Oddball Sessions

Jo Ann speaks:

Because we are often working in an atypical fashion, drawing in guidance and messages from Spirit, it's likely that some things that show up will be unanticipated, unusual, or even unruly! Sometimes that's because the Guides themselves like to play with us. At other times, there may be surprises because folks who seek guidance don't always know what they're getting themselves into. As Rev. Suzanne DeWees explained in an earlier chapter, this is not what you'd call a, "Dial-a-Spirit" service. If you specifically want a line out to your dead mother-in-law, you may need to learn channeling yourself. In the following pages, various channels check in, sharing strange or unexpected sessions they've experienced through their many years of practice.

I'll never forget a channeled session I conducted accidentally some ten or twelve years ago. It was while I was doing hands-on energy work and had just concluded a full Healing Touch session for a lovely woman from New York, whom I'll call Jeannine. As I sat in meditation, beginning to wrap up the session, I heard a very strange message. It came through loud and clear in my mind, and it was short and sweet—but unmistakable: "Tell her to sing!" I thought to myself that I must have gone over the edge. But again, the distinct message came through: "Tell her to sing!" So, I sheepishly walked around the table, and addressed Jeannine, "This may sound strange, but I've just received a message from Spirit that seemed important to pass on to you." "What is it?" she asked. And I repeated exactly what I had heard, "That I should tell you to sing!" Instantly Jeannine sat bolt upright and exclaimed, "Who told you that? Where did you hear that?' Shrugging my shoulders, I simply said to her, "It came to me from Spirit, while I was doing our closing meditation."

Copious tears fell as Jeannine explained to me that her beloved sister had died only eight months before, and they had been very close. Following that, Jeannine made a firm decision to stop singing. She was an opera singer, and she decided not to accept any more contracts or be part of any musical events. We spent a good amount of time processing that bit of news, and later on I was pleased to learn that Jeannine had gone back to her singing career—happy to receive her dear sister's advice.

Suzanne speaks:

Once in a blue moon I have an odd session. That was the case when an older woman came to me and wanted to know what kind of mistake she had made five years ago. I asked her to help me out—was this a mistake having to do with relationships? Her family? Or was it something related to her work or her finances? And she said to me,

"*You're* the psychic. You tell me!" I said to her, "Well, I am the psychic, and I'm asking you to leave…"

Very often my Guides do the heavy lifting at the beginning of a session. They'll start us up at a higher vibration; often they will provide guidance for the person and it's as if together we're building an energetic platform from which information flows. Very often at that point a deceased relative will show up. One time before I got ready to do a phone reading, a man with a red plaid shirt came into my awareness even before the phone rang. It turned out that he was the client's father, and he had arrived early, just waiting for the phone to ring and for her to be on the line. (And I wondered if her dad often had to wait for her back when he was still present in real life!!)

Marty speaks:

I don't know if you'd characterize this session as oddball or strange, but it was certainly out of the ordinary! You may remember the gentleman I spoke to you about earlier who had suffered great trauma and abuse in his childhood, whom we worked with to help allay the intensity of his PTSD symptoms. After a period of time I saw him again for acupuncture and pain relief, but this time for a different reason. He had developed such severe back pain that he actually needed surgery. As a result of that he had developed drop-foot and was moving toward long-term, severe neurological damage, so they did surgery and it helped a bit but didn't fully relieve the problem. He ended up with such severe pain that he yelled, "Get me to the emergency room." This happened frequently. In one session where he expressed fear that he was going to end up in a wheelchair for the rest of his life, we actually did some deeper work where he was able to make peace with the image of himself in a wheelchair. Not that he wanted to wind up that way, but he made peace with the fact that he would still be whole, wheelchair in his life or not.

Then he had this extraordinary experience, where he and his family were going by one of those drive-by birthday parties during the pandemic, and all of a sudden, his body started convulsing and twitching and going in and out of consciousness. They called 911 and got an ambulance right away. They rushed him to the hospital while telling his wife not to let him fall asleep. When he woke up in the hospital, he had a vision in which he saw a friend of his who had died. His friend said to him, 'You can come with me.' He was about to go along, when he looked back and saw his children and each member of his family bathed in beams of light. The whole thing was beyond extraordinary for him. When he finally woke up, the pain had left, he was completely restored, and he was at peace.

In the next session when we were together, I used the breathing technique to help him reconnect to that spiritual experience and anchor him in. So, he was doing the 4-8 breathing pattern as he relived that whole vision, and now he has that anchored in his system. It's not just a memory; it's something he actively uses when life gets stressful or difficult. Now he can go to that place that he had in that vision and with that 4-8 rate of breathing, he can become fully present and be at peace with himself.

Kathi speaks:

A young woman came for an energy healing session to release her anxiety and find ways to better manage a medical condition. In my practice I first close my eyes and tune into the person's energy field. Almost immediately the presence of a deceased soul got my attention and asked to communicate. My body was trembling with cold. As I turned my attention to the Spirit, I actually sensed the presence of male energy that was ice cold; there was literally no energy flowing through his etheric body. I described my impression to the young woman who began to cry. She explained that her brother had been found frozen to death in a snow bank a couple of months earlier. We had a beautiful healing conversation that brought great comfort and relief. It was as though our heads had been pushed together, while her brother's Spirit was laughing in the background. She informed me that her brother had been quite a jokester in life, and we knew then that he had made us bump noses. After that, we both continued laughing hysterically. Prior to that experience she did not believe in the afterlife, now, however, she knows that she has a true ally in Spirit.

Jo Ann speaks:

Perhaps the most oddball session of all was not even a *session*, as we might consider it. It happened years ago when I was still on Kripalu's faculty, leading a personal growth program called "Quest for the Limitless You." One bright day we transported our twenty guests to a local llama farm in Lee, Massachusetts and hung out together with the animals and with Dawn Costerisan, who happens to be an animal communicator. As we entered the llama pen, several of these dear creatures gathered around, curious to get closer to us.

The oldest and most benign of all the llamas, named Equalizer, slowly approached where I was standing. As I took out my camera, I said to Dawn, "Ooh, I hope I can capture him on film." At which point, Equalizer ran away. Puzzled, I turned to Dawn and asked, "Why did he escape so quickly?" To which she responded, "That's because you said you wanted to capture him on film! He didn't like the idea of being captured, no matter what way." Several members of our group burst out laughing. Soon Equalizer came back to join us as we formed a big circle inside the pen. Participants were encouraged to join hands on either side of the seven llamas that stood watching us, their beautiful eyes gazing at each person.

In typical program fashion, I invited everyone to meditate for a few moments. At the end, we chanted the sound of OM—the universal sound of peace. When we finished, Dawn approached to thank me for inviting her. She then addressed the group and me, saying, "The llamas appreciated your quiet time. And they told me that when you chanted OM at the very end, in that moment you became exactly like them!"

Chapter 12

The Choice is Yours

Jo Ann speaks:

Every day we wake up and are faced with multiple choices. Should I walk or meditate or perhaps do yoga practice? Should I pray or check my newsfeed? From daybreak to nightfall, from season to season, and from youth to old age, we are faced with multiple choices. Most of the time our lives follow such habitual patterns that we're hardly aware we've made a deliberate choice about anything. At other times, choices are made along the lines of what helps us avoid pain or bring greater joy into life. And when we explore the joy side of this equation, we observe how it often unfolds in sequences that coordinate and are aligned with our energy field and its various dimensions.

If you're acquainted with the chakra system, joy related to the root or first chakra could be summed up as a profound sense of belonging, being grounded, having the means to survive and feeling at home. Second chakra joys have to do with sensuality, sexuality and full use of your creative powers. So, moving through these layers, we find assorted joys and pleasures that make up the human experience. The more your choice reflects what's closest to your heart and soul's longing, the deeper and more profound your experience of joy and fulfillment.

On a mundane level, what choices need to be made this day? Is it time to post a letter, pay a bill, shop for groceries, or catch up with emails? Do you need fun, physical activity, or special time with your family? Then consider what choices are present that arise from even deeper longing—perhaps, from within your soul. You have free will and choice every moment that you draw breath. You can choose to live from dream or fantasy, from habitual pattern or brand-new exploration. When you study the chain of choices that give rise to your current life experience, you may begin to detect an over-arching pattern.

Consider further. Where have your key choices led you to in terms of relationship? Work? Living quarters? Learning? Adventure? Spiritual growth? What choices are up for you now that perhaps never entered your conscious awareness until this moment? As you evolve, things fall away that are no longer of great importance, while at the same time choices come more to the forefront that are a match to your evolving consciousness. When you sense that what you truly long for is matched up with your spiritual core and that you are clearly moving in that direction, then the next series of choices line up in a row like obedient little soldiers awaiting your command.

The Choice to Channel
Danielle Rama Hoffman

Southern France, 7/01/20

Danielle is an international coach and channel, keeper of the Ascended Master Lineage of Thoth, leader of the new paradigm of Unity Consciousness and successful spiritual entrepreneur since 1994. Three-time bestselling author of *The Temples of Light*, *The Council of Light*, and *The Tablets of Light*, she is the creator of Divine Transmissions, which supports conscious leaders, healers, coaches and mentors to create their legacy work (books, programs, businesses) with Source.

Danielle's clients embody their Divine Creator Being self, up-leveling their visibility, and birthing their highest-level contribution and legacy-work out into the world on a big scale. Learn about her retreats and high-level mentoring with Thoth, such as Divine Light Activation and Ascended Master Academy on her website: www. divinetransmissions.com

The Choice to Channel

Thoth speaks:

Hello, Dear Ones, this is Thoth with an expanded Council of Light moving into the forefront of this Divine transmission. We are delighted to contribute to this very rich conversation about channeling the sacred, for it is multi-dimensional in nature. What we wish to emphasize is the choice each of you has to partner with the Sacred, with the Divine, and with Beings of Love and Light. Choice is essential to this type of communication. We know that in a sense, you are always channeling the sacred. However, we are specifically focusing on the subject of this book, and the more conscious and deliberate process of channeling—of communicating with higher wisdom, frequency, and consciousness—while communicating with the Higher Self, with Beings of Light—with Guides.

To us, choice is one of the ingredients that is essential to this type of partnership. What we mean by *choice* is that you are engaging in a sacred partnership ignited out of your desire and your choice to enter into it. You are engaging your free will and your conscious choice. In this conversation, we are amplifying the energy of choice, for there are many, many misconceptions about channeling which ignore this key ingredient. When you choose, you are in the seat of Creator. When you choose, you are in the energy of Divine-to-Divine, and of equality and Equanimity—all essential to this process.

Choice is *ever present*, meaning that it's in every aspect of your channeling practice. It isn't a choice that's made and forgotten. Nor is it only in in one area; it is in all areas. You're at choice as to whom it is that you partner with among us Beings of Light. You are choosing what genre of material you may tap into. You are choosing to bring forward the channeled material of consciousness in a certain way. You are choosing how your particular channeling unfolds and is aligned for you. You are choosing *all* of it, and the full consciousness of choice implies an acceptance of the reality that you are Creator.

Part of choosing is *yes*—what you say yes to—and also *no*—what you say no to. One of the reasons that in the past you may not have fully chosen to ignite the entirety of your Divine capacity to channel is what we are implicitly speaking about by highlighting the energy of choice. We hear again and again that those who have shut down this communication to channel have done so because of the fear that if you were to receive certain guidance that you would then *have to* follow that guidance. That is not true. You are at choice all the way through. You are not only at choice; you are creating, you are co-creating, you are creating anew.

With this choice of *yes,* you receive information, guidance, consciousness, and then you choose to create based on the guidance you receive or you choose not to do so. So, we would invite you, if you are called—to make a choice—to be a *yes*. That *yes* entails making many choices, among which is to be a *no* for connecting with slower vibrational energies. When you make a choice to be a *yes*, if it is a *yes*, then know that we're only connecting to that which uplifts you and is an enhancement to you and to others. And that is the true basis for a sacred channeled experience.

All is light and love, and we are all.
Thoth and the Council of Light, as Divinely Transmitted by Danielle Rama Hoffman

Conclusion

Jo Ann speaks

Once upon a time the Buddha instructed his disciples not to get too caught up in his teachings, which might, in fact, interfere with their innocent or spontaneous engagement in life. He compared his teachings to that of a raft. While you're crossing the water, it is helpful to have something solid to ride upon. But once you're back on dry land (in other words, working from your own platform), then you no longer need the raft. Rely instead upon your own knowing and intuition.

Channeling, as a matter of fact, is a process of recognizing and becoming well established in the security of your connection. Danielle likens it to receiving a steady signal and finding ways to maintain it, in her words.

The Key to Receiving a Steady Signal from the Divine

Danielle speaks:

Acting on Divine Guidance to realize the next evolution of your vision can feel easier said than done. *What if I'm interpreting the download wrong? What if the timing isn't right? Who am I to show up this boldly?* The result is that you move forward at a snail's pace, second-guessing yourself at every turn and holding back the entire way.

For my clients and I, Divine downloads get a much different reception. Because our Divine Selves are in partnership with Thoth and the Council of Light to receive downloads direct from Source, we trust what comes through 100%. We don't doubt it at all. There's no questioning or overthinking, we easily access and choose to act on higher guidance without hesitation. Now, of course, we are ALWAYS at choice as to what we implement or not, based on what Thoth has just outlined for you earlier.

However, as fully embodied Light Beings Incarnate, we have this deeper knowing that makes it easy to receive, make decisions, and move forward without the old paradigm confusion that can stymie others.

Maybe you've experienced a glimpse of it? You know, in those moments that feel like the stars have aligned and your trust is all the way there and you act! Only, this way of moving in the world is difficult to maintain when you're trying to connect with the Divine and your Guides from the old paradigm. Rooted in Separation Consciousness, the old paradigm scrambles the signal you're receiving from the Divine with slower vibrations like doubt and second-guessing. It's like trying to listen to your favorite big city radio station while driving through the country. The radio signal is coming through, but there are times out in the boondocks where the reception gets spotty. The music starts to cut in and out and you find yourself struggling to decipher the tune instead of confidently singing along. What you need instead is a way to receive a steady signal that never cuts out so you can count on it no matter what. That way you get to keep humming along, no matter what environment you're in.

"The key to receiving a steady signal from the Divine lies in expanding into your multidimensional nature so that you can receive it, not from your old paradigm vantage point (where the signal can be spotty and hard for you to trust) but from the Unity Consciousness vantage point of your Divine Self. When you're able to do this, you receive guidance and you choose to act. There's no second-guessing or questioning required. You just know how to fully occupy your Multidimensional Leadership space and operate in a vibrationally conducive environment regardless of what's happening around you."

Receiving and Transmitting Light

The Guides speak:

Much of channeling, then, is taking in, modulating and re-configuring Light into words and concepts that make sense to others. Yet, it takes practice to get accustomed to this form of communication. Blocks of information readily pour in on the multiple light beams entering, but language is often a step down from the original intent. Yet there is power and potency in the message. You will often find amusement, delight, and true wonder. You may also find times you might define as wake-up calls, since the Light entering has the strange habit of altering everything in its path. Most importantly, it is altering your perception of yourself, of Life, and of Consciousness itself.

Often you may come out of a channeled session, realizing that you're different from when you entered. Channeling introduces enormous spiritual power into your life. In a sense it is asking you to get to know who you are ALL OVER AGAIN and at the same time get to know all the amazing Light Beings who're working with you!

Jo Ann speaks:

I love the way Thoth inspires us to continuously align our purpose and our practice with the best possible outcome for all involved, so then more and more becomes possible! We hold the energy, we make the choice, and that vibrational stance naturally raises the bar.

And so, we come full circle. As the author, I am delighted to have been in the company of such esteemed presences—such amazing, talented and generous souls who have gathered here providing so many beautiful messages to keep illuminating our hearts. Through days of wandering and writing, pausing, pacing and then perceiving, this channeling work has taken on a life of its own. It has created its own order, its own criteria, and its own explanations. In fact, it no longer belongs to me as the author, or even to my brilliant Guides. Nor is it the province of any one person or Being in Light.

As I mentioned in the very beginning, channeling is a communal experience. And once we recognize that we participate in a community that is both embodied and disembodied, then we can recognize how extensive and truly unlimited is our connection with and access to the Divine. As Thoth mentioned earlier, we are channeling the Sacred in every moment. All we really need to do is to wake up to that reality!

And now, Dear Ones, it's time to take up your sacred calling. Roll up your sleeves. Turn off the news. Take out your notebook or turn on the recorder. You have so much to look forward to! In the act of channeling, your presence itself illuminates and rearranges the field of Consciousness through which you transmit and receive energy. Channeling is thus an adventure of the highest order. Look upon it not as a task or challenge but rather as a grand gathering—or perhaps even a party! So much is already on its way to you; *laissez le bon temps rouler!* Let the Good Times roll!

Acknowledgments

For their wonderful words of wisdom, their separate commentaries and the unique spiritual technologies each of these contributors has developed, I wish to thank Rev. Suzanne DeWees, Ann Elliott, Marty Benjamin, Kathi Pickett, Dr. Jan Seward, Soleah Dance, and Danielle Rama Hoffman.

And I heartily thank my precious publishers, wordsmiths and designers, Michelle Vandepas, Gracie Packard, and Shauna Hardy for the ways they've *channeled* their own expertise. With their combined efforts, they've helped launch this work as a shiny satellite, traveling around, bringing Light into this world!

Needless to say, there is no way to thank all the extraordinary Beings of Light in Light who have been busy sending constant commentary from the Divine. To my Council of Light, I offer thanks, gratitude, and extreme homage.

Author Bio

As a longtime spiritual counselor and teacher, Jo Ann Levitt sheds new light on the ancient spiritual practice of channeling in her latest work, *Channeling the Sacred, Activating your Connection to Source.* A prolific author who has written on a variety of topics, Jo Ann was a senior Kripalu faculty member for thirty years and continues to teach meditation and provide spiritual counseling at Canyon Ranch in the Berkshires. She is also a licensed RN and Healing Touch practitioner. Jo Ann has learned from her years of channeled writing and spiritual practice that each of us is meant to be partnering with Spirit and participating in the co-creation of new and beautiful works for the benefit of humanity. Jo Ann considers herself one vehicle among many, as the work of co-creation is eternal and continually evolving. *Channeling the Sacred, Activating your Connection to Source* marks the fourth book in a series of channeled works that include *The Twenty-First-Century-Gospel of Jesus Christ*, its Spanish version, *El Evangelio de Jesucristo del Siglo Veintiuno*, and *Prayers for the Pandemic*, an anthology of prayers and poems centered on the challenges of these difficult times. For more information, please visit Jo Ann at https://joannlevitt.com/

For more information, please visit Jo Ann
Levitt online. joannlevitt.com

SCRIBES OF LIGHT
—— P R E S S ——

**Please find more channeled and inspirational
books from Scribes of Light Press.**

http://gracepointpublishing.com/scribes-of-light-press

Made in the USA
Monee, IL
16 May 2021